3Libertarian Essays

Daniel B. Klein

FEE Occasional Paper / One

The Foundation for Economic Education, Inc.

30 South Broadway
Irvington-on-Hudson
New York 10533
(914) 591-7230
Fax (914) 591-8910
E-mail:
freeman@fee.org
FEE Home Page:
http://www.fee.org

Founded in 1946 by Leonard Read, the Foundation for Economic Education (FEE) is committed to enriching people's understanding of the economic and ethical advantages of free markets, private property, and strictly limited government.

FEE seeks to improve the world not by taking sides in current policy debates but, rather, by educating people about the workings of free, private-property markets. To this end, we are committed to speaking and writing clearly and with energy, but never with rancor.

Like clockwork, liberty's opponents devise one false justification after another for interfering with the lives and properties of peaceful people. FEE tirelessly offers logical and historically compelling arguments against such falsehoods.

If FEE succeeds, the burden of proof which today is borne by those who oppose government intervention will shift to those who endorse political solutions to real (and imagined) social ills. Interventionists of all stripes will have a more difficult time peddling their schemes.

FEE's focus on education and what we call "the freedom philosophy" was explained cogently many years ago by Leonard Read:

> We do not tell anyone how to run his life; instead we try to explain how the open market process makes for harmony and peace. We do not look to the political process beyond the bare minimum of protecting life and property; instead we emphasize the harmful consequences of legal plunder. We take no stand on specific legislation; instead we set forth the broad principles that should underlie all law.

—Donald J. Boudreaux, President

The Foundation publishes The Freeman, *a monthly journal of ideas in the fields of economics, history, and moral philosophy. FEE also publishes books, conducts seminars, and sponsors a network of discussion clubs to improve understanding of the principles of a free and prosperous society.*

FEE is a nonprofit 501(c)(3) tax-exempt organization. It is supported only by the contributions of more than 10,000 individuals, businesses, and private foundations.

Libertarian
Essays

Daniel B. Klein

FEE Occasional Paper / One

The Foundation for Economic Education, Inc.
Irvington-on-Hudson, New York 10533

3 Libertarian Essays, by Daniel B. Klein

FEE Occasional Paper One

First published in April 1998

by

The Foundation for Economic Education, Inc.
30 South Broadway
Irvington-on-Hudson, NY 10533
Phone: (914) 591-7230
E-mail: freeman@fee.org

ISSN 1098-1276

ISBN 1-57246-100-4

Cover design by Beth R. Bowlby
Manufactured in the United States of America

Contents

About the Author

Daniel B. Klein received his bachelor's degree in economics at George Mason University (1983) and his doctoral degree at New York University (1989). By virtue of a postdoctoral award from the Institute of Humane Studies, he was visiting scholar at the economics department at Stanford University. Subsequently he was assistant professor of economics at University of California, Irvine. At Irvine he directed for four years the Liberty Society of Irvine, a student group and lecture series focusing on public issues and libertarian scholarship. He is now associate professor of economics at Santa Clara University.

Professor Klein's published works include *Curb Rights: A Foundation for Free Enterprise in Urban Transit* (Brookings Institution, 1997; coauthored with Adrian T. Moore and Binyam Reja), and *Reputation: Studies in the Voluntary Elicitation of Good Conduct* (University of Michigan Press, 1997; editor). He has published several professional articles on the private toll-road companies of nineteenth-century America, and professional articles on spontaneous order, coordination, discovery of opportunity, trust in markets, and the division of knowledge. He has worked and published with the Cato Institute, the Reason Foundation, the Independent Institute, the Institute of Economic Affairs, the Brookings Institution, and the Foundation for Economic Education.

Author's Acknowledgments

During the preparation of these essays, I received valuable comments from a number of individuals.

Go Ahead and Let Him Try: A Plea for Egonomic Laissez-Faire: David Boaz, May Cowen, Tyler Cowen, Walter Grinder, Thelma Klein, Tracy Krasnasky, Randy Kroszner, and D. McCloskey.

Liberty, Dignity, and Responsibility: The Moral Triad of a Good Society: D. McCloskey, Thomas Szasz, and especially Adrian Moore and Bob Higgs.

If Government Is So Villainous, How Come Government Officials Don't Seem Like Villains?: Milton Friedman, Amihai Glazer, Bernie Grofman, Daniel Hausman, Timur Kuran, Titus Levi, John Majewski, Miriam Schulman, Carole Uhlaner, two anonymous referees for *Economics and Philosophy,* and seminar participants at George Mason University.

In final preparation of this Occasional Paper, I thank Beth Hoffman for unfailingly attentive and cheerful assistance.

Preface

The three essays collected here originally appeared in disparate journals and are reprinted with changes. I am grateful to the Foundation for Economic Education for the opportunity to present them as a set. The first two papers explore the moral consequences of government policy. Those consequences are both personal, as the rules within which one lives affects the meaning of one's life, and political, as the character of a people affects the determination of policy, partly by affecting the extent to which justifications for policy become valid. The first two papers suggest that morals in society work with government policy as an interdependent system, a system which might begin steering itself toward results no one originally wanted. The third paper explores beliefs within government agencies. It too suggests that communities work by cultural systems and the yearning to find meaning in life. The papers suggest that liberty is the legal framework that best suits the meaning-seeking animal.

—DANIEL B. KLEIN
Santa Clara, California
1998

Go Ahead and Let Him Try: A Plea for Egonomic Laissez-Faire

At a sandwich shop I used to frequent in Cliffside Park, New Jersey, there was a video game—Galaga, I believe—with a sign on it saying, "Must be 16 years old to play." Evidently someone felt that video playing by "youngsters" was "getting out of hand." In truth, playing Galaga can, in the case of the skillful, consume a lot of time, and, in the case of the unskillful, a lot of time and money. It won't expand the mind, and the skills developed are unlikely to be of lasting service, except in playing video games. In favor, however, is the sheer joy of it—what else is life for?

Suppose we call in a cost-benefit analyst who follows the writings of Thomas Schelling. The analyst says: There are two utility functions to account for, the ephemeral utility function that enjoys the video game, and the enduring utility function that gets very little from the activity yet bears a cost in the form of forgone constructive activity. She reaches into her scientist cap and pulls out weights for each of the two utility functions, accounts for the corresponding costs and benefits, and comes up with a policy recommendation of whether to permit the activity. I submit that such a procedure overlooks something important.

For several weeks a certain high school freshman has been sharpening his Galaga game. He has learned not to neutralize all the alien-bugs so one may capture his fighter, which if then rescued delivers double-barreled firepower. No longer is his fighter destroyed by flies hovering treacherously at the foot of the screen. The boy has mastered the wiggles of the scorpion-trio

Reprinted with corrections and minor changes from *Inquiry: An Interdisciplinary Journal of Philosophy,* vol. 35, 1, 1992, pp. 3–20, by permission of Scandinavian University Press, Oslo, Norway.

and regularly picks up the point-blank bonus on them. The pattern of the first Challenging Stage is so familiar that he often polishes off all 40 bugs even with single firepower. This week he achieved a new personal best and now claims second position on the machine's record of scores. To the boy the game is a meaningful challenge and a basis for friendship among his peers.

Ignorant of the new ordinance he bikes down to the sandwich shop and discovers the sign on the machine. He asks the sandwich maker "Why?" and learns of the new law. Is this not a blow to his self-respect, an assault that can have lasting effect? The local authorities have told him, "trying to advance to the seventh phalanx of bugs is not the proper way to spend your time. You've behaved foolishly these past weeks, possibly reflecting a fundamental personal defect. It's time to shape up." The boy is demeaned—his notion of self-determination damaged—by the peremptory ability of the prohibitionists to strip meaning from his life.

He tries to forget the insult and decides to play anyway, thinking, "What are they gonna do, throw me in jail?" But the sandwich maker says, "You gotta be 16 to play. We can get a summons." Looking his age and having given it away by his earlier behavior, he decides nervously to finish just this one game. He doesn't even make it to the fifth phalanx. The machine is taken over by an older and much inferior player, and the boy looks on for a while. He has stopped playing Galaga. Being of tender years the boy lacks the confidence and worldliness to feel only contempt for his prohibitionists. The incident leaves him less sure about his instincts in spending his time and more apprehensive about his pleasures and challenges.

The literature on multiple selves—sometimes called "egonomics"—challenges one of the most basic precepts of economics: that the individual knows best in matters that concern her alone. If individual behavior consists of impulses that sometimes conflict, maybe the one that holds sway at a particular moment will do something regrettable. Even Robinson Crusoe generates externalities, as when he gorges himself with clams and fried coconut. Afterward one Robinson curses the now vanished glutton that left him with a bellyache, just as Pigou's laundry curses the factory.[1] The externality is internal. The presence of an externality brings to mind a second economic precept—that externalities may call for restriction—undercutting the precept of individual sovereignty. The inclination to use government measures to guard against internal externalities I (and Paul Heyne[2]) call parentalism.

A careful examination of the multiple selves literature turns up little of a parentalist flavor.[3] Perhaps a high respect for letting the individual play out her drama of self-control on her own accompanies a fascination with how people grapple with the problem. Thomas Schelling gives off a very faint (and very humane) parentalist glow when he writes about the "intimate

---

1. A.C. Pigou, *The Economics of Welfare* (London: Macmillan, 1960), p. 184.

2. "Most people would say *paternalistic*. But *parentalistic* is a more accurate and less sexist term." Paul Heyne, *The Economic Way of Thinking*, eighth edition (Upper Saddle River, N.J.: Prentice Hall, 1997), p. 370.

3. In their survey on intertemporal choice George Loewenstein and Richard Thaler say, "How can it be rational for a consumer to choose a refrigerator that costs $50 less than another equivalent model but consumes $50 more in electricity every year? While such cases do not establish a need for government intervention, the presumption that consumers choose best for themselves is rather weakened"; "Anomalies: Intertemporal Choice," *Journal of Economic Perspectives* 3 (1989). Thomas A. Barthold and Harold M. Hochman discuss parentalist policies in relation to their model of addiction; "Addiction as Extreme-Seeking," *Economic Inquiry* 26 (1988), pp. 102–05. See also Robert J. Michaels, "Addiction, Compulsion, and the Technology of Consumption," *Economic Inquiry* 26 (1988), pp. 85–86, and Tyler Cowen, "Self-Constraint versus Self-Liberation," *Ethics* 101 (January 1991): 360-73. In a brief discussion Jon Elster rejects parentalism, *Ulysses and the Sirens: Studies in Rationality and Irrationality* (Cambridge: Cambridge University Press, 1984), pp. 84–85. For discussions of the justifications of paternalism see John Kleinig, *Paternalism* (Totowa, N.J.: Rowman & Allanheld, 1984) and the collection edited by Rolf Sartorius, *Paternalism* (Minneapolis: University of Minnesota Press, 1983).

contest for self-command."[4] Schelling was more outspoken when he appeared on "The Today Show" in 1985 to comment on the federal excise tax on cigarettes. He advocated doubling the tax on a pack of cigarettes from 16 cents to 32 cents, because it would help people not to smoke. Schelling takes similar parentalist stances in an interview published in *Health Affairs* (1990).[5]

But regardless of what egonomists say about parentalism, the parentalist potentialities of egonomics are logically clear and routinely heard in policy commentary. The notion of rash and regrettable behavior helps to justify many laws in the United States. In most states one can suffer interrogation and a fine for motorcycling without wearing a helmet. Similar penalties are prescribed for unbuckled seat belts. Safety zealotry stands behind many of the "consumer protection" laws (in a recent effort to ban drain cleaners a lawyer said, "Using Lewis Red Devil Lye is akin to playing Russian roulette").

Indulgences in nefarious and supposedly self-destructive activities are guarded against. States have limited gambling to keep the poor from falling into bad habits. To help people preserve their self-respect and the family circle we have proscriptions on sexual graphics, commerce in sex, and certain bedroom practices. For those in a self-jeopardizing mental state, mental health experts help them, willy-nilly, through tough times. Laws help prevent the abuse of a wide variety of substances, from heroin to antibiotics. Laws also limit the advertising of liquor and tobacco.

---

4. See Thomas C. Schelling, "Egonomics, or the Art of Self-Management," *American Economic Review* 68 (1978), pp. 290–94; "The Intimate Contest for Self-Command," and "Ethics, Law and the Exercise of Self-Command," both in his *Choice and Consequence* (Cambridge: Harvard University Press, 1984). In the last, for example, one gets the feeling that Schelling might favor a mandatory delay procedure for getting a tattoo, which he describes as a "permanent mutilation" (p. 105). On the other hand, in the essays on organized crime (chaps. 7 and 8), Schelling's words have a certain libertarian resonance.

5. "Perspectives of an Errant Economist: A Conversation with Tom Schelling," interviewed by John K. Iglehart.

Many laws supplement the wills of young people: there is physical education in school, in case they neglect to exercise; there is school, in case they neglect to think. Child labor laws help young people escape wage slavery, and ordinances like those of Cliffside Park aid them in managing their time wisely. As they reach adulthood and begin to earn their keep, Social Security helps them overcome the impulse of racing through their earnings and arriving at a state of insolvency.[6] Other laws protect them from buying on impulse, from hiring unqualified plumbers or therapists, from marrying someone who is already married, from murdering themselves. These restrictions are not justified solely on parentalist grounds.[7] But inasmuch as they are, the parentalist offers the restriction as a service to the erstwhile partaker.

Schelling's program of self-control is primarily tactical, the message being that "some intriguing parts of strategic self-management are like coping with one's own behavior as though it were another's."[8] Well, Schelling's program is a nice aid, but if it turns out to be insufficient in subduing the Mister Hydes that lurk, perhaps the government can lend a hand. After all, subduing bad guys is what the government is all about.

Schelling says that he is not talking about "the development of inner strength, character, or moral fiber."[9] It is to Schelling's credit that he can treat the matter of self-control so searchingly while avoiding "anything mysterious or philosophically pro-

---

6. Laurence J. Kotlikoff presents paternalism as a leading argument for Social Security, saying, "[f]or all such myopic, misinformed, miscalculating, and lazy households, government-forced saving and insurance purchase through Social Security . . . may be highly beneficial." In his conclusion he says, "empirical evidence . . . suggest a basis for paternalistic concern about inadequate savings and insurance"; "Justifying Public Provision of Social Security," *Journal of Policy Analysis and Management* 6 (1987), p. 689.

7. Several of the restrictions described are defended with the charge-of-the-state argument: people must be restrained because the cost of catastrophe falls on the community chest. Being bound collectively by the long fingers of the welfare state, we must bind ourselves individually with seat belts.

8. Schelling, "Intimate Contest," p. 63.

9. "Intimate Contest," p. 69.

found." But "the development of inner strength" (which in truth Schelling is getting at) may be a point worthy of concern.

The undying nature of the egonomic challenge leaps from Schelling's prose. Nevertheless there prevails a tendency, even among Schelling readers, to think of conflicting selves as special cases. Some people concede that unsmoked cigarettes swirling down the toilet and Christmas Club savings accounts are striking cases, but feel that the idea doesn't extend too much further. How far the idea extends matters when thinking about parentalism. If regrettable behavior arises in isolated and identifiable ways, more or less uniformly across individuals, then a helping hand from the government may be just the thing. If regrettable impulses are pervasive and personal, and the ability to deal with them is an art that applies beyond specifics, an art that is learned and strengthened through exercise and a sense of autonomy, then the parentalist hand needs to show its own restraint.

———

In a social milieu where many relationships intertwine, out of common purpose or propinquant convenience, there often develop vague notions of propriety that express themselves in *shoulds* and *shouldn'ts, supposed to's,* Good and Bad. Drugs are Bad, work is Good. Too often the consensus accords, for focal point reasons, with whatever is passed down from official opinion headquarters.

But even the defender of the official theory of Good and Bad is left with a world of unprejudged options to steer through, trying to do the right thing at the right time in a very particular world only he, and sometimes a spouse, knows. The day is a constant motion through rapids, around bends, always surprises around the corner. To hang on we fall back on our impulses. But our impulses do not always steer us through, or, at any rate, not to the satisfaction of a later us. To discriminate unfailingly between our impulses on the spot, for a remote voice, larger than the waves and bends, to guide us always, is the dream we all dream of. But, on the spot, is this dream a guiding angel, or just another impulse, albeit a better one?

In bed, Sunday morning, cares for the day come to mind. Let's get things done! Searching for resolve I head for the grapefruit juice, but on the way slip on a grease spot: the morning paper, a cafeteria of easy amusement. Two hours later I try to recall the first care on the list. Some people spend hours every day following the press. A simple pleasure, we might say—some deem it productive for the valuable knowledge it bestows. Could be, but for some I'd call it addiction. The spouses, children, and pets tend toward this view. Books are surely a Good thing—isn't reading the first purpose of primary school? Still there is excess, "the bibliobibuli . . . who are constantly drunk on books, as other men are drunk on whiskey. . . . They wander through this most diverting and stimulating of worlds in a haze, seeing nothing and hearing nothing."[10]

If the country's leading addictions call for an official campaign, I propose the following slogan: Just Say No to Sports. We've got 17 weeks of football, college and pro, plus the bowl games, about 30 weeks of basketball, and about the same for baseball. There is professional hockey, soccer, golf, bowling, boxing, track and field, autoracing, and gymnastics. The irresolute can get on a wheel a year in circumference and never get off. The wives tend toward this view. But, hey, what about the thrill of the kickoff return, the sublime beauty of the opposite field base hit, the complete catharsis of one fighter driving another to the mat? Sports are a leading source of beauty and drama. For most American males the role of sports as social glue is probably second to none, and the sheer joy of it is probably second to one, or two. So lay off. Still, I know more than one person who wonders why he bothers to look at the lifeless denouement of nine-to-nothing ball games and messages from the sponsors.

Like sports, minus the grace and nobility, is politics. Around campaign time many people become fanatical for political news,

---

10. H.L. Mencken, *Minority Report: H.L. Mencken's Notebooks* (New York: Alfred A. Knopf, 1956), p. 59.

including people who ought to know better. I am often amazed to learn of apparently sensible people solemnly taking in the soothing platitudes of politicians, whether Republocrat or Demopublican. In this case, however, people do not display much regret, in consequence, no doubt, of the outward legitimacy of the addiction.

Even *supposed to's* can be bad impulses. Paying the bills is Good. But we can fritter away important blocks of time by listening too closely to "Take care of paperwork" impulses. We've got to discriminate even when all the likely options are Good. We are hatched with a stock of impulses, many of them troublesome and unbecoming, that we learn to subdue. We cultivate a richer array of impulses and empower them, through reflection and exercise, to come forward at the appropriate time.

And time isn't the only casualty of regrettable impulses. Schelling has described a vast array of egonomic challenges that, if handled badly, can mean financial, professional, or personal setback. And sometimes financial or professional advancement is the addiction. The attaining of something eclipses the thing itself. Earning money eclipses enjoying the things money buys. I am not speaking of creative passion or even the simple pleasure of carrying a project to completion, but mere compulsiveness. I refer to the pious turners of fast bucks, the promoters of efficiency at all cost, the strategy infatuates, and the vitae vikings. In like fashion I refer to the die-hard dusters and spongers, the feverish bundle-uppers, the politeness hounds, the crack-brained fixers, the insatiable conservationists, the somersaulters for safety, and the pixilated logic-choppers. Sometimes we revel in our compulsion and wouldn't dream of surrendering a bit of it. Sometimes we wonder why the less fervent corners of life, perhaps our health or domestic joy, are growing musty.

As you see, two can play at the game of pejorative flinging (pejoratives like "addiction," "drug abuse," "irrational," "compulsion," and a battery of psychiatric terms that demean[11]). Part of

---

11. See Thomas Szasz, *The Second Sin* (New York: Doubleday, 1973), pp. 20–22, 26, 31–32, 64, 70–76, 119; and *Heresies* (Garden City, N.Y.: Anchor Press, 1976), pp. 36–42, 137–38, 145–46.

my point is to suggest the vast similitude of all peaceful habitual activities, namely the human effort to elude boredom. Also, I hope to suggest the depth of self-command.

In a split second a mischievous smile can ruin the mood for an entire evening. Many of us will agonize for weeks, months, even years over a cogent demonstration of our obnoxiousness, wishing we could take it back. Sarcasm that's meant to wound is often regretted, as are pestering and teasing, arrogance and snideness, deceitfulness and trickery, interrupting and abruptness, humiliation and intimidation, complaining and criticizing, shouting and swearing, slapping and kicking.

If we are awake we know that every impulse has its regrettable moments. Sometimes we would like to take back having worked overtime, having pulled our weight, having been forgiving, having *not* slapped or kicked. The impulse of conciliation may lead one into cowardice, helpfulness merges subtly with toadyism, and the wholesale repression of sarcastic and derisive impulses, especially at an early age, may strand the individual in the slippery chute that empties into conventional thinking. There is great danger in making a habit of caution. Every turn presents a chance for regret.

The course never gets more perilous than in the torrent of love, where basic impulses often find themselves in conflict. Propping up faith in the fairy tale of love while salvaging independence and self-respect is, for many, an impossible feat of navigation. In a song entitled "Two Faces" Bruce Springsteen sings of an inner foe that rebels against the fairy tale. Permit me all five verses:

I met a girl and we ran away
I swore I'd make her happy every day
And how I made her cry
Two faces have I

Sometimes mister I feel sunny and wild
Lord I love to see my baby smile
Then dark clouds come rolling by
Two faces have I

One that laughs one that cries
One says hello one says goodbye
One does things I don't understand
Makes me feel like half a man

At night I get down on my knees and pray
Our love will make that other man go away
But he'll never say goodbye
Two faces have I

Last night as I kissed you 'neath the willow tree
He swore he'd take your love away from me
He said our life was just a lie
And two faces have I
Well go ahead and let him try

———————

When we are engaged it is an ephemeral self, an impulse, maybe several, that is scurrying to handle the business. *I* has eyes on but not hands on the business. *I* is the captain (or, if you like, the soul), confined to a gray room, only a few inches from one side to the other, and equipped with an enchanted violin. He plays tunes that magically summon and set to dancing a crew of pulsing helpers. They perform the tasks, including the thinking. They feel the world, hear its noises, taste its flavors, but their experiences echo back to the captain in the gray room. Through memory the captain relives the echoes. In solitary moments when the impulses are retired—lying in bed awake, meandering through the hills on a still afternoon, settled behind the wheel on a long, lonely drive—the captain nearly sees the sun.

The captain aspires to travel certain courses—to write the book, to build the home, to carry on as a nonsmoker, to be a gentleman. In the small his missions are from A to B—perhaps the port of impetuosity to the port of better manners. In the large the captain makes his journeys to trace out a self-portrait in the expansive waters. His ship is like a woodcarver's knife. It is not a portrait of who he is but of who he wants to be. With his enchanted violin he tries to find the tunes that get his crew to cooperate.

The captain does not page through a wish book and order up the self-portrait of his choice. His journeys are continually adapted from where he has been, both because his history shapes his wants and because his history shapes the inclinations of his crew. The crew, as Schelling has made clear, are not mere puppets asking to have their strings pulled. They often have an agenda of their own. Perhaps these impulses were well adapted to a *former* self-portrait, perhaps one of the absurd and beautiful self-portraits of youth. Or perhaps these impulses took shape at a time of sleep for the captain, when there was no course, when the bundle of impulses just took cover from a barrage of instruction from outside. Now these unwanted impulses have become habits. Each impulse now feels entitled to its own little turf. The captain faces a formidable task in subduing and disarming these impulses, just as a statesman or executive faces a formidable task in crushing entrenched interests to get his government or organization on the right course. Through determined reflection the captain searches for the resolve to turn out his obstructive impulses, sometimes taking the form of Schelling's tactical warfare. Only through conscious effort does he find a new tune on the enchanted violin. Only over time can a habit be supplanted.[12]

We may never achieve all the features of a projected self-portrait. Ask a smoker if she would welcome a tiny detector, implanted in the arm, that would zap her with pain if she lit up but would otherwise be unnoticed. She knows that it is removable only at considerable trouble and that it would prevent her

---

12. My captain-crew metaphor is akin to the more technical metaphors of Richard H. Thaler and Hersh M. Shefrin, "An Economic Theory of Self-Control," *Journal of Political Economy* 89 (1981), pp. 392–406, and Gordon C. Winston, "Addiction and Backsliding: A Theory of Compulsive Consumption," *Journal of Economic Behavior and Organization* (1980), pp. 295–324, and to the less technical metaphor of Walt Whitman, "That Shadow My Likeness" [1860], *The Portable Walt Whitman* (New York: Viking Press, 1973), p. 201.

from smoking. With the zapper her existing "Let's light up!" impulse is overmatched by her "Keep that #$★%&!@ pain out of my arm!" impulse. If, after deliberation, the smoker chooses the zapper, then in this matter she has trouble managing herself. Her ship is not tracing out the desired self-portrait. If, on the contrary, the smoker declines the zapper, she is, on the whole, happy as a smoker (although she still may smoke too much, since the zapper offers only all-or-nothing alternatives).

What do we want to be? In Harry Nilsson's tale *The Point!*, everyone in the Land of Point has a point on the top of his head (except Oblio). To produce, to join, to believe. We could all produce more, we could all rise to greater heights in our arena. Schelling gives the example of the Hungarian radical Georg Lukacs, who was magnificently prolific thanks to house arrest.[13] If "output" is society's goal, maybe we should incarcerate more writers. Obviously we want time for amusement, time to loaf, time to celebrate. We feel most alive when we find combinations of activities that are compatible, cohesive, and challenging.

We may not be everything we would like to be, but the ship sails on and a portrait is traced. Often we struggle and fret to become what we are, and are proud of it. Once we have cultivated the impulses to maintain a self-image, plying along on the same course, retracing the same portrait, becomes more relaxed. But when we will not settle for what we are we have to work on managing ourselves, we have to combat our habits. What makes us want to improve our self-portrait? How do people depose the entrenched impulses? And what makes people joyful in being who they are?

When Gargantua asked Friar John Hackem, who had shown good sense during the Cake-Peddlers' War, to govern the Abbey of Seuilly, of Bourgueil, or of Saint-Florent, the friar refused, demanding, "For how could I govern others, who cannot even

---

13. "Ethics, Law and the Exercise of Self-Command," p. 91.

govern myself?" The friar consented to founding his own community, the Abbey of Thélème, where the motto was *Fay ce que vouldras* (Do as thou wouldst).[14]

Such humility is rare, especially in those with political prerogative. As a sovereign one could accommodate an orgy of elaborate impulses. Whether bleeding the subjects would be a matter of remorse depends on the sovereign's character. In the film *The Private Lives of Elizabeth and Essex,* Essex chose death over life because life would mean supreme power, by virtue of bonding with Elizabeth, and supreme power would mean the pursuit of conquest and the ruin of England. He saw in a brave moment the hubris that would prevail.

Hubris breeds regret and in turn an awareness of the need for better self-command. We believe much too readily that when we come to "that bridge" we will remain faithful to the design we now hold. We forget that life is a series of overlapping but separate and often quite engrossing aesthetic experiences, that the mood and vision in which plans are laid may vary greatly from the moods and scenes experienced as the course is traveled. Beforehand we say we won't gamble it all, we won't get angry, we won't watch TV, we won't crash the ship on the rocks, we won't, we won't! I say I won't indulge myself in a book all evening and neglect the dishes, but in the morning we have to look at a pan of crusty, cat-licked spaghetti sauce. For a long time I said I wouldn't drive fast, I wouldn't! But I advanced to "Driving Safety" school none the less. I have learned to seek a car with a manual transmission and a small engine because they disarm my dangerous and otherwise supreme impulse to speed excessively ("dangerous" because of the chance of levies by the highway patrol and allied agencies). My impulse to speed is fully armed and aroused by my motorcycle, but I take a dubious pride in saying that I am free from hubris in this regard— not because I don't speed but because I have surrendered completely to the impulse. O how it basks on the 405!

---

14. Rabelais, *The Portable Rabelais,* Samuel Putnam (ed.) (New York: Viking Press, 1946 [1533]), pp. 198–200.

People discover their hubris and learn how to lessen it not by a compulsory diet of Sophocles, but by experience. Although hubris is like a bull terrier, people who want to overcome it learn to after repeated failure, embarrassment, and regret. In my line a common hubris we learn to overcome is that of perfect recall. Many are slow to realize how fleeting a valuable idea can be. Our first disposition, it seems, is that what we see clearly in the mind's eye now we will see clearly at the appropriate moment in the future. When we sit down to "write it up" it will all come back. Then we finally confront that terror and our mind is nearly blank, just two or three stray ideas are adrift. In terms of impulses the hubris is a rationalization for a "Leave me alone I don't want to make notes and files" impulse. The struggle during the terror teaches us something for next time.[15]

Sometimes it is not our own outrageous fortune that sets us in search of better impulses, but the pleasing fortune of someone else. We see someone perform deftly in the sort of situation we usually perform poorly in, and think, "I'd like to learn to do that." Nothing awakens our soul like the image of one we admire. Sometimes the contrast between ourselves and the foil just screams at us to revise ourselves. What these situations are, and what our shortcomings are, are so special, so particular, so personal, that only we can sense the lesson that another's example teaches. Trying to impart deftness of any but the most formulaic sort by uninvited instruction is unlikely to succeed:

> Examples draw when precept fails,
> And sermons are less read than tales.[16]

In fact, overinstruction can turn precepts into mental prophylactics and numb the soul. Here we have a sort of moral

---

15. As does reading Donald McCloskey's *The Writing of Economics* (New York: Macmillan, 1987), pp. 13–15.

16. Matthew Prior, *Poems on Several Occasions,* 1708.

application of Hayek's principle about the knowledge of time and place.[17]

Turning out an unwanted habit can be quite a battle. We may need to psych ourselves up, to build a vigilance. We mythologize the importance of self-reform. A parent says, "If I criticize him I will lose his love and deserve to lose it." To learn to buckle up I told myself that if I don't buckle my seat belt I am not being fair to someone. By finding meaning in the self-improvement we nurture a new impulse, an impulse crafted to war on the entrenched impulse. The unfolding of the matter—sensing our shortcoming, reflecting on its nature, molding a new impulse, empowering it to surge forward at the right moment—gives a touch of drama that makes us rejoice at success. It is a real challenge and a real accomplishment. The interest in reforming ourself and the ability to do so are things that outsiders cannot enhance, but can diminish.

We are all authors of a sort. Of all the legends, tales, allegories, fables, anecdotes, and biographies we take in, none commands greater empathy than our own. The setting is gritty and real, the details are many and charming, the cast immense, the characters alive, the plot . . . well, the plot may not be as firm as George Lucas's or even Mark Twain's, but it is of our own authorship.

The helm is ours to command, to become what we want and what we can. May every captain cultivate a crew elaborate, competent, and happy! But measures like "Must be 16 years old to play" do not bolster the captain's confidence and may actually damage it. Virgil said: "They are able because they think they are able." Parentalisms tell them, "you are not able," and thereby may make them unable.

---

17. Friedrich A. Hayek, *Individualism and Economic Order* (Chicago: University of Chicago Press, 1948), p. 80.

Europeans are often startled by the drinking habits of American college students. In Greece, where alcohol is available to all, teenagers drink wine as their parents do. Treating someone like a child may induce him to behave like a child. There may be two Nash equilibria: one in which the individual is treated like a child and behaves like a child; another in which the individual is treated like an adult and behaves like an adult. A parentalist restriction selects the first equilibrium, which is probably suboptimal and certainly distasteful. In the film *Mary Poppins,* Jane and Michael write an advertisement for a nanny (which their father tears up) reading, "If you won't scold and dominate us / We will never give you cause to hate us." Sociologists' "expectation theory" or "labeling theory" says that people tend to fulfill the role others expect of them.[18]

When choices are made for us we fall into habits we know not why. Our impulses just go day to day without ever passing the captain's circumspection. Our activities do not have a larger meaning. We can march around in a bureaucratic stupor, where each impulse has its sacred little turf. Wean a person in a world of decrees and proscriptions and he may fear life beyond the bureaucracy. When government yelps out Rights and Wrongs, and enforces obedience, people may figure that the government—or Opinionators of a hundred sources and varieties—can do the choosing for them. They make a habit of letting others shape their habits.

There will be some who resist. Without a seat belt law I am proud of my habit of buckling up. With a law I am proud of not buckling up. A similar effect operates for drug use or suicide. With the law I have to ask myself, If I buckle up is it because I have come to my own conclusion that it is a good idea, or because I do as I am told? The second possibility repulses me. If I buckle up a doubt remains. If I don't, I ask myself, is it because I just don't care to or is it because I refuse to obey? So either way

18. See Robert Rosenthal and Lenore Jacobson, *Pygmalion in the Classroom: Teacher Expectation and Pupils' Intellectual Development* (New York: Holt, Rinehart, and Winston, 1968); and Robert K. Merton, *Social Theory and Social Structure,* revised and enlarged (Glencoe, Ill.: Free Press, 1957), pp. 430–36.

there is doubt; but in the latter case the doubt is between two more acceptable possibilities. Similarly, when a husband orders his wife to be loyal, the wife might disobey just to eliminate the possibility in her mind, and his, that he can command obedience. Prohibiting an activity is a sure way of providing a good reason to do it. Defiance is the self-respecting reflex to tyranny.[19]

Prohibition may create another motive for partaking. Schelling has pointed out that people may flout self-imposed rules not because they succumb to temptation but because they rush for "freedom from suspense, freedom from indecision, . . . from perpetual unfinished decision."[20] In the culture that grows like vines on the trellis of prohibition people may have to endure a similar suspense, the question of whether to "try it." People might try it just to relieve themselves of the perpetual unfinished decision. And trying it may not be understood as a mere relief, a mere peccadillo. The embroiling of the activity by prohibition may mean that the individual takes the decision to try it as a shameful brand and is ready to fry in hell. The experimenter is immediately a drug abuser, the adventurous wife is immediately a slut. "All Right! Persecute me!"

Prohibition may eliminate the temptation of nefarious activities, but it doesn't eliminate hubris. It doesn't confer a personal ability for steering a wise course in bewitching circumstances. Just as self-respect cannot be placed under a Christmas tree, self-command cannot be instilled by prohibition. Do we want to live in a society where our fellows are compelled to be Good, or where our fellows feel that they are one of a kind, their lives their own making? In "A Speech for the Liberty of Unlicensed Printing,"[21] Milton wrote:

---

19. In one of his papers having nothing to do with egonomics, however, Schelling gives a subtle and plausible argument why we might welcome laws mandating the use of hockey helmets, motorcycle helmets, and seat belts; "Hockey Helmets, Daylight Savings, and Other Binary Choices," in his *Micromotives and Macrobehavior* (New York: W.W. Norton, 1978), esp. p. 224.

20. "Intimate Contest," p. 81.

21. I find this quotation opposite the title page of *A Plea for Liberty: An Argument Against Socialism and Socialistic Legislation,* Thomas Mackay (ed.) (New York: D. Appleton, 1891).

If every action which is good or evil in man at ripe years were to be under pittance, prescription, and compulsion, what were virtue but a name, what praise could be then due to well doing, what gramercy to be sober, just, or continent? . . .

They are not skilful considerers of human things who imagine to remove sin, by removing the matter of sin; . . .

Suppose we could expel sin by this means; look how much we thus expel of sin, so much we expel of virtue: for the matter of them both is the same: remove that, and ye remove them both alike.

In a too-neglected statement of the personal dimension in political philosophy, Wilhelm von Humboldt said, a society "in which the citizens were compelled . . . to obey even the best of [behaviors], might be a tranquil, peaceable, [and] prosperous [one]; but it would always seem to me a multitude of well-cared-for slaves, rather than a nation of free and independent men."[22]

Coming to face one's hubris, being aware of our impulses, wanting to learn from example, wanting to make and meet challenges, enjoying what we are—these abilities run deep. They meet a thousand opportunities. They are not like algebra or good penmanship, mere skills of crew members. Our society emphasizes the proficiency of certain crew members, but shows disregard and even disdain for the captain's proficiency on his enchanted violin.

Hubris did not conquer Ulysses. But had Ulysses known a world girdled with parentalisms he would have been stripped of

22. *The Limits of State Action,* J.W. Burrows (ed.) (Cambridge: Cambridge University Press, 1969 [1791]), p. 79. In *On Liberty* [1859], J.S. Mill praises von Humboldt's emphasis on personal development and makes individuality a primary value in his discussion. Alexis de Tocqueville makes some characteristically beautiful remarks on this theme; *Democracy in America,* 2 vols. (New York: Alfred A. Knopf, 1945 [1835/1840]), II, pp. 336–39, 347; he also makes pertinent observations about the self-reliance of women in America, II, pp. 209–11.

his self-command. His ship would have been lost at sea, and with it a tale worth believing in.

Without pretense to any fundamental principle from which wise social policy can be derived, let me share a conviction which I think can bear usefully on matters of parentalism (as well as other matters). It is the Pantagruel Code:

> Social decency and good conduct show themselves most unmistakably in a readiness to spare others of shame and to preserve their dignity.[23]

True social decency does not dwell on, pity, or patronize someone's weakness or disadvantage, real or supposed. It does not rescue when rescue has not been sought. It does not judge or even draw attention to. It proceeds on the assumption that the individual is conducting his affairs as he sees fit, no matter how mad the method may seem. It in no way questions the captain's command.

Some may point to extreme cases to show that the Pantagruel Code is not a complete guide. They might conjure the image of the heroin addict, who has no self-respect to preserve, who cannot control his behavior. He is like a scratched record. The needle just keeps repeating, never getting out of the same horrible groove, never progressing in life. Surely a shove on the needle is justified.

Even for the posited extreme cases we have to ask: Are they really so horrible, really so much worse than the hidden and hellish cage we continue to know as year chases year? Are the extreme cases really numerous? Can the government really help

---

23. See H.L. Mencken, *Notes on Democracy* (New York: Alfred A. Knopf, 1926), pp. 172–75; H.L. Mencken, *Minority Report,* pp. 231, 233, 211; and Albert Jay Nock, "Pantagruelism" [1932], in Charles H. Hamilton (ed.), *The State of the Union: Essays on Social Criticism* (Indianapolis: Liberty Press, 1991). In "The Gay Science" (1882) Nietzsche wrote, "What do you consider most humane?—To spare someone shame" (Aphorism 274).

them? What else must we endure if we set up a government machinery to deal with the extreme cases? Even for the extreme cases I am inclined to hold the line, invoking the Albert Jay Nock Principle: If those actually involved can stand it, so can I.[24] If someone really is in a horrible groove let him reach out to friends, family, or a support group. If he fails to, is he worth rescuing? A grandmother I know has her own way of putting the Albert Jay Nock Principle: Everyone has a right to go to hell in his own toboggan.

———

I have spoken of the personal aspects of parentalism. Before withdrawing, let me mention other reasons to reject parentalism.
——

A friend of mine going back to grade school lives in Greenwich Village, works on Wall Street, and has done his share of cocaine. Several years ago at about the highwater mark of his rate of cocaine consumption I tried out my theory on him that half the allure of doing cocaine was in the illicitness—the adventure of procuring it, the signal it sends to companions, especially young ladies, the discretionary power in sharing it, the in-ness of having to keep a watch out, the naughtiness of partaking, the renegade delight in experiencing its effects—in brief, my theory that prohibition was the soil out of which ritual sprouts. I said that if cocaine were as legal as mayonnaise, and bore a similar price, the spice would be removed, the ritual would fade, and his usage would in a short time discontinue altogether. He laughed and said I was probably right.

In his book, *The Long Thirst: Prohibition in America, 1920–1933,* Thomas Coffey remarks: "It is appallingly ironic, however, that the same methods which totally failed to suppress

24. I am unable to relocate this passage in Nock's writings. In Nock's article "On Doing the Right Thing," he says: "The practical reason for freedom, then, is that freedom seems to be the only condition under which any kind of substantial moral fibre can be developed." *The State of the Union: Essays in Social Criticism,* Charles H. Hamilton (ed.) (Indianapolis: Liberty Press, 1991), p. 323.

alcohol, which on the contrary stimulated its greater use, should now be employed against narcotics."[25]

——

Some of our prohibitions have effects like those witnessed during Prohibition, which H.L. Mencken summarized in 1928: "Its damages widen and multiply. It has corrupted the police almost everywhere; it has prospered and encouraged criminals; it has brought religion into politics; it has sowed bitter and relentless hatreds. The Federal courts, once remote and impeccable, already show its smirches. . . ."[26] And defining certain peaceful activities as crimes means a reallocation of public resources. As Thomas Szasz observes, "the more politicians protect people from harming themselves, the more they fail to protect them from being harmed by others."[27]

——

Justice in this country is little more than a word, and one of the reasons is parentalism.[28] Parentalism contributes to the erosion of sound norms of justice. I may be an extreme case, but to some extent others share the sensibility that the enforcement of seat belt laws, of video game ordinances, of drug prohibitions, of school attendance, of child labor laws are less than noble duties. When I see on the roadside, as I occasionally do, the police frisking some poor Joe, hunched over the trunk of a car, sometimes a gun pointed in his direction, my instinct is not that justice is being served. The police are the bad guys. And my reaction is not so eccentric. The respect for the police (and public attorneys and judges) has been declining steadily and has almost gotten to the point where moviegoers feel compromised by a premise of a cop earnestly fighting crime. If a sense of privacy leads one to regard

25. (New York: W. W. Norton, 1975), p. xi. See also Mencken, *Notes on Democracy*, pp. 162–63.

26. H.L. Mencken, *On Politics: A Carnival of Buncombe,* Malcolm Moos (ed.) (Baltimore: Johns Hopkins Press, 1956), p. 217.

27. *Heresies,* p. 77.

28. An indictment of our institutions of justice is made by Bruce L. Benson, *The Enterprise of Law: Justice Without the State* (San Francisco: Pacific Institute, 1990).

the enforcement of parentalism as distasteful, the symbols of justice are stained. Public support for the police slips even when they are engaged in apprehending actual criminals. Of course parentalist restrictions are not the only dubious duties that the police must assume—I shall spare you a list—but parentalist restrictions represent a sizeable and highly visible chunk. The effect on the self-image and morale of the police and the court workers cannot be good, which further reduces public esteem. Parentalist laws contribute to the stoogification of our guardians of justice.[29]

Then there is the impact on the norms of wrongdoing in your neighbor's mind. Selling candy is basically a peaceful and useful service. So is selling cocaine. But selling cocaine is an illegal and (therefore?), according to many people, immoral activity. So is mugging and house-breaking, according to them and me. The sound normative distinction between selling candy and mugging is a shade less distinct. In the evolution of norms of acceptable behavior we cannot expect the preservation of perfect logic. Schelling remarks:"a large number of consumers [of black-market services] who are probably not ordinary criminals—the conventioneers who visit prostitutes, the housewives who bet on horses, the women who seek abortions—are taught contempt, even enmity, for the law by being obliged to purchase particular commodities and services from criminals in an illegal transaction."[30]

I don't doubt the sincerity and good will of Thomas Schelling when he advocates doubling the excise tax on cigarettes, but voices like Schelling's are seldom met with in the world of policymaking. In practice, parentalism is mainly a fraud. Let me state the Mencken Thesis. In his denouncements of Prohibition Mencken often put forth his conviction—a sincere and studied one, I believe—that uplift and do-gooding of that sort was rooted mainly in: (a) envy, and (b) a yearning to run things,

---

29. On the stoogification of judges, see Mencken's "Justice Under Democracy," *Prejudices: Fourth Series* (New York: Knopf, 1924), pp. 85–102.

30. "Economics and Criminal Enterprise," *Choice and Consequence,* p. 177.

to satisfy one's ego by harassing one's fellow humans. Karl Kraus, who had much to say about both (a) and (b), remarked: "Sensuality is oblivious of what it has experienced. Hysteria is obsessed with what it has not."[31] Regarding (a), note that it is never the motorcyclist who piously wears a helmet that pushes for helmet laws, and the opponent of other-than-missionary sex is rarely suspected of missionary gusto. After (a) and (b) we can add: (c) compassion posturing, made glamorous (in some circles) by certain dogmas (just as libertarian dogmas make glamorous posturing as a defender of "individual rights"); (d) mere political opportunism, whether vote buying (conspicuous in Social Security and child labor laws), revenue enhancement (conspicuous in sin taxes and the government gambling monopoly), or issue making (conspicuous in drug demonology). Finally, trailing far behind in blood and bone but leading the parade in effigy is: (e) sincere, good-natured altruism. The Mencken Thesis is that (e) accounts for no more than three percent of the animation for uplift.[32]

If the Mencken Thesis is true, and especially if it is true and not recognized as true, then there is real hazard in having parentalist palliatives floating free, like circus balloons in the tent of policymaking. It's-for-their-own-goodism will be invoked by political operators in Washington, Sacramento, and City Hall when putting through a piece of plunder or oppression. Better

---

31. See Thomas Szasz, *Anti-Freud: Karl Kraus's Criticism of Psychoanalysis and Psychiatry* (re-issue) (Syracuse: Syracuse University Press, 1990), p. 153.

32. "Mencken Thesis" is a term of my invention; see Mencken's "The Anatomy of Ochlocracy" [1921], in *H.L. Mencken's Smart Set Criticism,* William H. Nolte (ed.) (Washington, D.C.: Regnery Gateway, 1987), esp. pp. 154–56; "Moral Indignation," in *A Book of Calumny* (New York: Alfred A. Knopf, 1918), pp. 23–26; *Notes on Democracy,* pp. 35ff, 155ff, 176ff; *A Carnival of Buncombe,* p. 164; *Minority Report,* p. 261. In the second volume of his memoirs, Mencken did dub his own Mencken's Law: "Whenever A annoys or injures B on the pretense of saving or improving X, A is a scoundrel"; *Newspaper Days* (New York: Alfred A. Knopf, 1941), p. 38. Szasz makes many remarks in tune with the Mencken Thesis, principally elaborating on item (b); see *The Second Sin,* pp. 33, 46, 57, 65, 120, 121.

to wipe It's-for-their-own-goodism off the scrolls of political justification.

———————

Of Schelling's many vivid examples, one of the most illustrative is the plight of Captain Ahab, whose preservation depended on having his whale-bitten leg cauterized without anesthesia.[33] I like to think that I would help the shipmates pin down Captain Ahab as he resisted the hot iron that was applied to his bloody stump. I would hope they would pin me down if the bloody stump were mine. Likewise I subscribe to parentalism when it comes to toddlers who march off coffee tables and fall headlong into your arms, grinning; or friends, or strangers, in really exceptional circumstances of confusion, emotional debilitation, or intoxication. Of course.

But as a matter of social policy, I see a line here, a glimmering and protruding line, a line worth consecrating.

———————

33. "Ethics, Law and the Exercise of Self-Command," p. 83.

Liberty, Dignity, and Responsibility: The Moral Triad of a Good Society

In *The Constitution of Liberty,* Friedrich Hayek wrote, "the belief in individual responsibility . . . has always been strong when people firmly believed in individual freedom" (1960, 71; see also 1967, 232). He also observed that during his time the belief in individual responsibility "has markedly declined, together with the esteem for freedom." In surveying the twentieth century, noting the ascent of the philosophy of entitlement, the philosophy of command and control, and their institutional embodiments—the welfare state and the regulatory state—one can only respond, "indeed." Lately, perhaps, a reversal has begun.

We might advance the reversal if we better understood responsibility and its connection to liberty. We speak often of responsibility, but vaguely, even more so than when we talk of liberty. When Hayek refers to "the belief in individual responsibility," does he mean the striving by the individual to be admirably responsive in his behavior, to be reliable, dependable, or trustworthy? Or does he mean the belief that individuals ought to be held to account, to be answerable or liable for their actions? A drunken watchman can be held accountable for trouble that occurs during his shift; he is then both irresponsible and responsible. Indeed, the two kinds of responsibility tend to exist together, but they are conceptually distinct. As moral philosophers, we usually have the reliability notion in mind; as political philosophers, the accountability notion. To make the terminological distinction clear, I shall call the personal trait of being admirably responsive *personal responsibility,* and the social-

Reprinted with changes from *The Independent Review,* Vol. 1, No. 3, Winter 1997, pp. 325–351, by permission of The Independent Institute, Oakland, California.

relations trait of holding the individual to account *individual responsibility.*

Individual responsibility fosters personal responsibility. Policy affects morals. And personal responsibility enhances the appeal of individual responsibility and of liberty. Morals affect policy. Putting policy and morals together, we get feedback loops and multiplier effects.

I shall attempt to clarify the moral dimension of our statist ways. But moral philosophy here is handmaiden to political philosophy. I do not aim to persuade the individual to find or affirm certain moral outlooks or personal habits. I aim to persuade members of the polity to change government policy. One of the most important, if subterranean, arguments for changing government policy, however, is that doing so affects individuals' moral outlooks and personal habits, which in turn affects. . . .

Clarifying Liberty and Individual Responsibility

My usage of *liberty* has a common recognition and acceptance. By liberty, I refer to property, consent, and contract. By property, consent, and contract, I mean what traditional common-law conventions have meant. Of course, there are gray areas here—what is the precise scope of private property rights? what of implicit terms in agreements?—and one must consider the senile, children, and other hard cases. But as a famous jurist once said, that there is a dusk does not mean there is no night and no day. Some things are gray, but most are either black or white. Despite its areas of ambiguity, the principle of liberty is cogent and well established. In the United States it is most consistently and most completely espoused by the libertarian movement. National and state policies that clearly encroach on the principle of liberty include drug prohibition, drug prescription requirements, drug approval requirements, restrictions on sexual services, licensing restrictions, wage and price controls, health and safety regulations of private-sector affairs, antitrust policies, import restrictions, laws against discrimination in private-sector

26

affairs, and gun control. On the truly local level, such policies might be viewed as acceptable because we might grant town government the status of contract, as for a proprietary community. The point here is not that liberty is everywhere good and desirable, only that it is reasonably cogent.

Let us think of liberty as conceptually distinct from individual responsibility. Libertarians often speak in terms of the liberty dimension, disregarding the responsibility dimension. The point is familiar with respect to the welfare issue. The taxes, which libertarians may deem an encroachment on liberty, are only part of the complaint. Suppose that instead of our current national and state welfare systems, we had the following: governments at the national and state levels continued to collect the same taxes but instead of providing welfare payments, they gathered all the tax dollars into a huge paper mountain, doused it with gasoline, and set it on fire. This hypothetical arrangement encroaches on liberty just as much as the existing system does. Libertarians may instinctually prefer the bonfire, but they cannot explain this preference with reference to the liberty dimension. The government distribution of welfare payments is itself objectionable, and for reasons aside from government ineptitude. The difference between the welfare system and the bonfire lies in the dimension of responsibility.

We can analyze government policy better by distinguishing liberty from individual responsibility. The dole is one thing: that the dole is financed by confiscatory taxation is another. Historically and practically, however, liberty and individual responsibility are intertwined. They are, especially, morally intertwined.

"Individual responsibility" means accountability; more specifically, it means *government-administered* systems of accountability for citizens. Both liberty and individual responsibility, then, pertain to the citizens' relationships with government. Hence, in my usage, one citizen's crime against another is not an encroachment on liberty, and the practices of a philanthropic organization, even if arbitrary, are not departures from individual responsibility. I shall sometimes abbreviate "individual responsibility" as just "responsibility."

Think of liberty and responsibility as one-dimensional continuous variables. For the sake of setting the benchmark, we can describe the absolute liberty and absolute responsibility that constitute the Libertarian Utopia. Absolute liberty would be the freedom of property, consent, and contract among private parties. Government would maintain and enforce the legal order and not burden citizens with tax levies beyond those necessary to pay for these protective services. This arrangement is the classical Nightwatchman State, the utopia of Wilhelm von Humboldt, Frederic Bastiat, Herbert Spencer, William Graham Sumner, Albert Jay Nock, and other classical liberals. Here the government holds people accountable for their transgressions of property, consent, and contract—punishing criminals, enforcing restitution where possible, and adjudicating a thick-skinned tort doctrine—but it provides no other benefits to citizens. (Again I hedge on the question of local government because local government services beyond the Nightwatchman functions may occupy a gray area between ordinary contract and state power.) In the Libertarian Utopia, summarized in the middle column of figure 1, the variables "liberty" and "individual responsibility" both have their extreme values.

Departure from responsibility—indulgence—takes various forms, as summarized in the first column of the figure. In interactions between citizens and government, government acts with indulgence when it gives benefits to citizens—welfare payments, medical care, housing, schooling, freeways, and so on. In its policing of interaction among private parties, government engages in indulgence in making inadequate punishment of criminals (meaning burglars, not pot dealers). In its adjudication of civil disputes, government engages in indulgence by failing to make tort judgments against truly malfeasant defendants or by making tort awards to frivolous plaintiffs, for example, in liability, discrimination, or sexual harassment suits beyond the bounds of a thick-skinned tort doctrine.

Encroachment of liberty—coercion—takes the forms of confiscatory taxation (in excess of funding the Nightwatchman),

	INDULGENCE Departures from Responsibility	LIBERTARIAN UTOPIA Nightwatchman State	COERCION Departures from Liberty
Govt. Practice in Govt.-Individual Interaction	welfare-state benefits; free govt. services	taxation to finance the nightwatchman state	confiscatory taxation; conscription
Govt. Practice toward Private Activity	inadequate punishment of consent violators	freedom for consensual and protection from nonconsensual activities	restrictions, regulations, or prohibitions on consensual activities
Govt. Practice in Civil Disputes	frivolous awards to plaintiffs; failure to make judgments against malfeasant defendants	thick-skinned tort doctrine	frivolous judgments; failure to make awards to aggrieved plaintiffs

Figure 1. Departures from Responsibility and from Liberty, in Relation to the Libertarian Utopia.

conscription, any kind of restriction on consensual private activity, excessive punishment of criminals or detainment of suspected criminals, making frivolous judgments against defendants in civil disputes, and failing to make tort awards to truly aggrieved plaintiffs in civil disputes. (Again, these delineations apply in the context of state and national government; at the level of truly local government, the contours of liberty and individual responsibility are much fuzzier.)

Having clarified the concepts of liberty and responsibility, let us now consider their interdependence.

Interaction Between Liberty and Individual Responsibility

Government must be small and circumspect if society is to enjoy a high degree of liberty and a high degree of individual responsibility. To explain the magnitudes of these two variables in terms of the people's general attitude toward government— by whether or not they view it as wise and efficacious—we might say that liberty and responsibility vary together because they depend alike on the popular attitude toward government. Where people distrust government, they choose politically to have much liberty and much responsibility. A serious shortcoming of this approach, however, is that most people lack cogent views in political philosophy. Rather, their views on public issues are, if existent at all, superficial, inconsistent, piecemeal, and highly fickle.

Taking a more marginalist approach to the interaction of liberty and responsibility (economists might call it "comparative statics"), one asks: How do marginal encroachments on liberty affect responsibility? And how do departures from responsibility affect liberty? I shall briefly mention the more obvious connections only, then take up some subtler morals-based connections.

Before proceeding, however, we should acknowledge another dynamic: diminutions of liberty today can lead to further diminutions of liberty tomorrow, and likewise for responsibility. Recognized aspects of this dynamic include the slippery slope, the force of precedent—"How come they have protection from discrimination and we don't? How come they get subsidies and we don't?"—lock-in and status-quo biases in government policy, the prehensile government agency, the ratchet effect, and the intervention dynamic (Mises 1978, 75ff; Ikeda 1997). These factors help to explain how liberty and responsibility, each as a historical variable, undergo self-reinforcing changes—hence the famous saying of the Revolutionary Era about eternal vigilance being the price of liberty. A fuller treatment of how liberty and responsibility evolve through time would include discussion of these recursive processes. Here the focus is on how liberty and responsibility influence *one another* over time.

Much of the connection is direct and obvious. Welfare benefits and free government services, listed in the left column of figure 1, must be paid for by confiscatory taxation, listed in the right column. A similar direct symmetry appears in the bottom row, with regard to government practice in civil disputes: frivolous awards to plaintiffs imply frivolous judgments against defendants.

Other connections flow from the political economy of the matter. Commentators often point out the public-charge connection between diminished responsibility and diminished liberty. If taxpayers pay the doctor bills for repairing the motorcyclist's fractured skull, then there is a reason beyond parentalism for requiring him to wear a helmet. This argument arises often, in matters ranging from drug use to schooling. Hayek (1960, 286) not only acknowledged the point, he *employed* it in calling for a requirement that individuals purchase insurance for "old age, unemployment, sickness, etc." (though he opposed a unitary government institution). Thus, by accepting restricted individual responsibility as a premise, Hayek concluded by endorsing an encroachment on liberty.[1] The same dynamic appears in the argument that immigration must be curtailed because the newcomers expand the costs of welfare programs. A similar dynamic appears to have been at work in the Scandinavian states that engaged in forced sterilization, "to spare the state the heavy cost of providing welfare for the backward and frail" (Wooldridge 1997, M1).

Other political-economy connections also exist. In *The Road to Serfdom* (1944) Hayek explains that government planning necessitates encroachments on liberty and departures from responsibility, as the planning promotes the breakdown of the rule of law and the expansion of arbitrary government. Thus,

---

1. Note, however, that Hayek (1960) uses "liberty" a bit differently than I do here; see esp. pp. 20–21 and 142–44.

"the more the state 'plans,' the more difficult planning becomes for the individual" (76). Government's operation of the school system, for example, may well lead to restrictions on *private schooling,* in order to keep "the plan" viable. Government often favors its indulgence programs by hobbling the competition.[2] Thus, departures from responsibility lead to encroachments on liberty. Another connection ties the breakdown of the tort system to the rise of regulation (Wildavsky 1988, chaps. 4, 8); again the result is encroachment on liberty. In general, a breakdown of the rule of law leads to encroachments on liberty. Once individual responsibility loses force, liberty can turn into a riot of license. A stark example is the curfew imposed during actual urban riots. The influence runs in the opposite direction as well: restrictions on liberty cause poverty or the suppression of voluntary institutions, leading to government programs to supply what has been suppressed.

Clearly, liberty and responsibility exhibit acute fragilities, vulnerabilities, and instabilities. Yet none of the foregoing considerations takes into account the moral dimension, where we find an affinity between the morality of indulgence and the morality of coercion.

A Ship of Selves, But a Single Captain

Thomas Schelling (1984, chaps. 3, 4) has portrayed the individual as a bundle of multiple selves, often in conflict. Schelling describes how one self can foil another by acting strategically. The long-term self that wants to quit smoking might foil a short-term self by flushing the unsmoked cigarettes down the

---

2. A fine example comes from the making of Social Security in 1935. Senator Bennett Clark proposed an amendment that would give companies and their employees the liberty to opt out of the public program by setting up a parallel private pension. But Senator Robert La Follette explained that such liberty would not be tolerated by the new indulgence scheme: "If we shall adopt this amendment, the government . . . would be inviting and encouraging competition with its own plan which ultimately would undermine and destroy it" (quoted in Weaver 1996, 47).

toilet. The long-term self that wants to keep his wife makes heartfelt promises to be more attentive. We all experience regrets and the tribulations of self-command. Is each of us merely a bundle of ephemeral impulses ever struggling among themselves for control without an inner judge? I think not.

For when we reflect on our behavior, we may find it coherent, even spiritually moving. Certain impulses receive inner support or admiration. Thus, it may be that when we are tranquil, our true self, an inward eye, tries to sort out who we are and who we ought to be.

If only it were so. For when we examine the inward eye— with an eye yet further inward?—we find that it also is multiple and constantly in self-conflict. Our most personal reflections, most searching judgments, most decided resolutions are—*yet more impulses!* Perhaps the impulse to smoke belongs to a dual long-term self that wants to be the being that certain exciting achievements enable him to be, and those achievements can come only from the steady nerves that smoking a cigarette affords. Perhaps the impulse to neglect one's wife belongs to a dual long-term self that wants ample freedom to pursue dangerous adventures, to complicate and enrich life's loves. Even our thoughts are actions of a sort, carried out by impulses or selves. True, they are impulses operating at a deeper level, perhaps with a powerful influence over whole sets of shallower impulses, yet somewhat alien and suspect nonetheless. We cannot escape bitter struggle and sorrow even within the deepest level of consciousness.

Must we endure an amoral existence, the product of a mere struggle of opposing forces based on historical contingency, none worthier than the rest? No heroes to root for, no romances to experience, just hungers in conflict and transient gratifications?

Perhaps not. First of all, no one ever said transient. Some sentiments breathe and rejoice for a lifetime.

As for *worthiness,* even here we need not surrender. If consciousness, even in its farthest reaches, cannot reveal to us reliable indications of the worthy, let alone the worthiness algorithm itself, we still have the subconscious. After all, the conscious must emerge from somewhere. Even within economic philosophy, Michael Polanyi (1958) tells of tacit or inarticulate knowledge, which forms the roots of our ideas and the basis of our beliefs, and Israel Kirzner (1985, chap. 2) describes entrepreneurial discovery, a component of human action that is motivated but not deliberate.

But in the realm of tacit knowledge and the subconscious, do we again find multiplicity and conflict, a lack of unitary *essence* telling us what is worthy? Must we reach yet farther to satisfy our yearning for a sense of worthiness that guides our actions and gives meaning to our lives? How do we ever come to say that a story has a moral?

In the end we come to a fundamental question of existence, to which the answer must be action, not explanation. Time to act. If we must, let us believe in the soul. If the soul does not exist, let us invent it. A sense of worthiness is itself worthy. I simply affirm that I belong—my soul belongs—to the force for affirming the sense of worthiness and meaning. Happily, you belong to that force, too.

The ship of selves, then, is in the hands of a multitude of crew members, each trying to pull the ship's course this way or that—or neglecting it altogether—to satisfy its special limited desire. But the ship's course results not merely from this diffuse process of conflict and negotiation among crew members. There is also the captain. Though he keeps to his cabin below deck, he works his influence on the crew members. Some he feeds; others he starves. Some he tutors into new becomings, refining them to specialized tasks for specialized moments. He cajoles and disciplines, hoping to get them to work together. He is constant. He wills but one thing. He has a destiny, ever distant, and he strives to manage the crew so as to follow the course that now seems to him best calculated to make his approach. He is neither Good nor Bad; he simply is. His being makes things good or bad. He judges worthiness and he gives meaning to the journey.

Some may rejoin, "What a plush tale you tell! And what

34

makes it so? What evidence can you give? You offer us *mere* myth."

Myth indeed, but better a myth than a vacuum. For this myth is *worthy*. And I doubt that anyone will dispute its worthiness.

The plea is to try always to end on a note of hope of character integration. Figure 2 (on the next page) shows the spiral of disintegration and reintegration of character. On top are notions of the integrated self. The arrows on the right side bring the disintegrative challenges of multiplicity and inner conflict. The arrows on the left side affirm a deeper resolution, restoring integration. The spiral shows the soul as the limit, impossible to reach or reveal, and shows that being human has two sides: one to be accepted candidly for the reality it is, the other affirmed and made real by hope, struggle, and pain. The two sides, left and right, of figure 2 coincide with the "two different sets of virtues" described by Adam Smith:

> The soft, the gentle, the amiable virtues, the virtues of candid condescension and indulgent humanity, are founded upon the one [namely, the set of virtues that pertains to the arrows on the right side of figure 2]: the great, the awful and respectable, the virtues of self-denial, of self-government, of that command of the passions which subjects all the movements of our nature to what our own dignity and honour, and the propriety of our own conduct require, take their origin from the other [namely, the set of virtues that pertains to the left side of figure 2]. (Smith [1790] 1976, 23)

I use the metaphor of the ship crew to represent self-multiplicity and conflict at one level, and that of the ship captain to embody the integrative force of a deeper, encompassing self. This crew–captain relationship is recursive; hence "the captain" is not the soul, but merely the hope of progression to character integration and, for the time being, resolution.

35

Self-Esteem, Self-Respect, and Dignity

The feeling of self-esteem is one of good cheer among the crew in action, of solidarity among themselves, of satisfaction and pride in the ship they serve. It often comes from outward recognition of achievements to their credit. Although self-esteem comes from positive reinforcement, the feeling is always somewhat illusory, for self-satisfaction naturally fuels self-striving. Self-esteem occurs at the shallow levels of the ship of self, and fluctuates with the ebb and flow of achievement and recognition. A compliment from an admired soul will send it soaring; a criticism or rejection will make it sink.

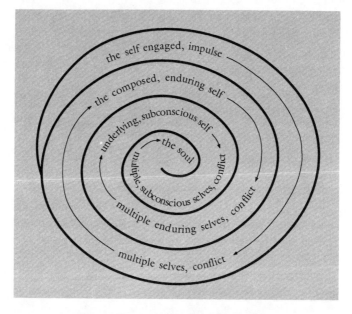

Figure 2. The Spiral of the Self: Disintegration
and Reintegration of Character

Self-*respect* runs deeper. John Rawls (1971) speaks of two aspects of self-respect. "First of all, . . . it includes a person's sense of his own values, his secure conviction that his conception of the good, his plan of life, is worth carrying out. And second, self-respect implies a confidence in one's ability, so far as it is within one's power, to fulfill one's intentions" (440). We might interpret as follows: First, self-respect requires a feeling that one has a coherent moral force within oneself, that the judging faculty—the captain—exists. Second, self-respect requires hope among the crew that the captain can maintain his command and keep his mission alive. Together these two elements cause the crew to respect the captain. Out of respect, a crew member will sacrifice himself in response to the captain's will. Personal responsibility is a corollary of self-respect.[3]

But a respectful crew member does not always feel good cheer in his work. There can be respect without esteem. The crew member might question, negotiate, or even rebel. Inner conflict, turmoil, and inconsistency belong to a process of regeneration of the crew, a process of self-search and self-creation. "A foolish consistency is the hobgoblin of little minds" (Emerson 1951, 41). The captain's will to travel ever onward might mean that some crew members who have served their function must now be disposed of, and they, being habits of the mind and the heart, will resist. Inconsistency, disappointment, disillusionment, and pain accompany self-search, the process of reaching back to find a deeper understanding that will reconcile or resolve conflict. The search may yield the disappointing discovery of one's limitations—so some crew members in charge of hope must die—or the terrifying resolution that the hopes can live but only by the grueling sacrificial slayings of other parts that are old and dear. From the search for self-respect comes both gratification and despair.

A steady feeling of self-esteem, or satisfaction, is not possible for the normal aspiring person, so it is not any sort of ideal. Unflagging self-respect may be an ideal, but self-respect is an attitude about oneself projected inward, so it is not generally possible or even meaningful for an observer to gauge self-respect in others. Self-respect remains very personal and individual.

---

3. The discussion here has been influenced by the chapter entitled "Dignity, Self-Esteem, and Self-Respect" in Murray (1988).

Individuality makes like actions differ among individuals; in each case the action plays a unique role in a unique story. Self-respect is a question not only of our own voyages, but of our own destinations.

The observer cannot peer into the private ocean of another, but the observer can gauge the extent to which someone comports himself in relations with others so as to afford himself self-respect. In a word, we can form an idea of the extent to which the individual comports himself with *dignity*. Dignity is a social phenomenon. It is not about how one behaves in the exclusive company of oneself, but about one's outward behavior in relations with others.

We value dignity in our fellows because their example and standard aid us in behaving with dignity ourselves, which helps us to respect ourselves. By behaving with dignity, we take possession of ourselves, sort out our impulses, measure the worthiness of one impulse against another, clean ship if necessary, and on the whole give ourselves a more coherent and enduring sense of mission. The captain nourishes the crew members, but he is nourished in turn by them.

Let us place dignity then in the footlights along with liberty and responsibility. Dignity measures a certain quality in the behavior of the members of the society. That quality has two aspects: first, the extent to which they guard their own self-respect, or preserve their own dignity, in their social behavior; second, the extent to which they accommodate the self-respect of others, or preserve the dignity of others with whom they interact.

In preserving our own dignity, each of us says:

> My struggles are a necessary part of me, emerging from my personal drama. You may hear a crew member indicating a desire to be treated in a belittled fashion, but *now* I indicate that I will welcome no such treatment. I have validity and method in my being; don't tread on me. My drama is *mine*. I am its author and judge. I create its meaning. By showing self-possession, I show that

38

I *possess* my story, and therefore you do not. It is my *property,* and you have no right to use it for your purposes except with my welcome and *consent,* in which case I make interaction with you part of my being.

In preserving our own dignity, we affirm the myth of the captain and his mission. We oppose those who would use our being without due regard for our own story, our own meaning. In preserving dignity, we oppose those who would demean us by denying, disdaining, or belittling the captain, the integrative moral force, of our being.

In acting so as to preserve the dignity of others, we presume that the individual is conducting his affairs as he sees fit, no matter how mad the method may seem. We respect his individuality. We do not dwell on, pity, or patronize someone's apparent weakness or disadvantage. We do not attempt to rescue when no rescue has been sought. We do not judge or even draw attention to, except insofar as doing so is a part of the relationship the other has willfully entered into. We honor an ethic of MYOB—Mind Your Own Business. We in no way question the captain's judgment or his command. Acting so as to preserve the dignity of others might also be called acting with common decency.

The relationship between the two aspects of societywide dignity—guarding one's own self-respect and accommodating the self-respect of others—will not be considered here, but it would seem that the two go hand in hand, based on a sense of universal human likeness, or brotherhood.

Although liberty and individual responsibility have been defined narrowly within relations involving government, the same political orientation does not hold for the definition of societal dignity. I am considering dignity as exhibited by individuals throughout society, in all sorts of social interaction.

Dignity is a worthy goal for a political or social movement, perhaps the worthiest. But my present goal is not to celebrate dignity or to recommend a plan for its achievement. Rather, I have introduced dignity to show the moral mechanism linking liberty and responsibility. If liberty and responsibility each have a reflexive relationship with dignity, then they have a reflexive relationship with each other.

The Interdependence of Dignity and Liberty

If the individual consists of multiple selves, the question arises: Should the government protect Dr. Jekyll from Mr. Hyde, just as it protects the innocent citizen from the criminal? If the individual is multiple, then in a way his actions are not so personal after all. One self imposes an externality on other selves, and externalities raise the issue of whether the government ought to intervene. Americans commonly make the assumption that intervention is called for with regard to opium use, gambling, Social Security, safety issues, suicide, and many other matters.

But the support for parentalism rests not only on the notion of the multiple self, but on the presumption that the conflict among the selves represents a sort of moral collapse. It is rather analogous to butting into a domestic dispute. A married couple needs to learn how to respect and tolerate one another, their dispute belonging to the drama of their marriage. In the case of the multiple self, the parentalist solution can make sense only once the hope for self-respect is lost. The parentalist presumes that the crew has taken over the ship, that all respect for the captain is lost and the crew no longer responsive to him. Dignity is gone. It is time, reasons the parentalist, to sacrifice liberty as well.

Thus, low societal dignity leads to coercion. The less the citizen preserves his own dignity, the less it makes sense to say that he acts in keeping with the captain's mission. Such doubt about individuals' mastery over their own behavior is manifest in the war on smoking waged by David Kessler, the former U.S. Commissioner of Food and Drugs. He views the decision to smoke as resting in the hands of tobacco companies. Owing to their practices, he says, "Most smokers are in effect deprived of the choice to stop smoking." Part of the reason Kessler is prepared to doubt the dignity of the people is that, in fact, their dignity is not as high as it might be. For example, John Gravett (1993) wrote a

40

magazine column titled "Life-Long Smokers Should Welcome Hillary's 'Nico-Tax.'" Gravett declares that the First Lady's tax hike of two dollars per pack "will surely bolster my resolve to quit." "I, like so many other life-long smokers, am only waiting for a good enough reason to quit once and for all" (54). Rather than searching as an adult to come to terms with his habit, Gravett glibly asks that he (and all other smokers) be treated as a helpless child. Citizens such as Gravett lend truth and legitimacy to Kessler's presumptions.

Low societal dignity motivates Kessler's actions in another sense, too. Dignity has two sides. Kessler himself reflects low societal dignity in the sense that he is loath to preserve the dignity of others by accommodating the self-respect of smokers.

Kessler's attitude typifies what Thomas Szasz calls the therapeutic state (1963, 212–22; 1990, 253–61). Viewing personal behavior in terms of health and medical conditions, agents of the therapeutic state quickly attribute an individual's troublesome impulse to forces outside his moral being. Rather than seeing the impulse as a test of the captain's mastery over his crew, they see it as a sea monster that has attacked the ship and now must be cast off. Viewing the problem as caused by an alien force, they fancy themselves saviors stepping in to subdue the alien by restricting its powers. Rather than viewing the enjoyment of gambling, opium, or tobacco as growing out of and belonging to the being of the individual, they view it as an "addiction," an illness or disease that, like the mumps or smallpox, has descended on the individual and now warrants "treatment." Insofar as the prohibitionists regard the "illness" as a permanent constitutional condition, a "sick" part of the being, their coercive ways signal their disdain for the validity of the captain.

If eroded dignity leads to erosions of liberty, so too does eroded liberty lead to erosions of dignity. Parentalist prohibitions and restrictions flatly tell the individual: "You are not competent to choose fully; we must circumscribe your choice." As Isaiah Berlin (1969b) puts it, "to manipulate men, to propel them toward goals which you—the social reformer—see, but they may not, is to deny their human essence, to treat them as objects without wills of their own, and therefore to degrade them" (149). Parentalism very plainly declares that the captain is invalid or incompetent.

Thus, the individual is invited to play the role of a child, unable to manage himself and unqualified to judge for himself. The individual must either accept the role set out for him or willfully resist the culture that presses him into that role. Such resistance can be psychologically arduous. In the culture of parentalism the childlike role creeps up on the citizenry, compromising their dignity. Individuals begin to surrender the romantic idea that the captain is the source and author of one's own meaning. Hence parentalist encroachments work to demean the individual's existence. This is the most tragic consequence of parentalism. Here I wish to submit a new term, to stand for the process and consequence of citizens being demeaned by social practices and institutions (and I wish the term weren't so ugly—although, an ugly name suits the beast): *demeanedization* (pronounced de-mea-NED-ization). Although one of the important consequences of parentalist policies, such as drug prohibition, Social Security, and occupational licensing, is demeanedization, that consequence is very rarely noted in debates over such policies.

With the affront to dignity comes a loss of personal responsibility and self-possession. Berlin (1969a) explains:

> For if I am not so recognized, then I may fail to recognize, I may doubt, my own claim to be a fully independent human being. For what I am is, in large part, determined by what I feel and think; and what I feel and think is determined by the feeling and thought prevailing in the society to which I belong. (157)

Psychological research supports Berlin's claim (Rosenthal and Jacobson 1968; Merton 1957, 430–36). Parentalism demeans its subjects and becomes a self-fulfilling prophecy.

Parentalism demeans people in other ways as well. It treads on individuality. The habit of gambling, drug use, or leaving seat belts unbuckled may not even be a personal problem, a point of inner conflict. Many people roll the dice, snort, or smoke in moderation; they have no misgivings whatever about their actions. Yet parentalism tells them that the activity is bad, and therefore demands that everyone fit a common mold. "But I am an individual; I have made myself unique," responds the miscreant. Again, resistance is psychologically arduous and, weary of resisting, the individual succumbs and dignity suffers.

Parentalism also damages dignity by the brutality of enforcement. Even those who successfully reject the morality and culture of parentalism may taste the bitterness of enforcement. Detainment, questioning, handcuffing, strip searching, and imprisonment are brutal, dehumanizing experiences and, whatever one's political views, bound to challenge one's belief in one's own mastery over existence.

As Lord Acton's maxim reminds us, power tends to corrupt. Parentalist encroachment damages dignity also by rehearsing the parentalist in denying dignity to others. Coercing people at one place now, the parentalist learns to treat them with small regard for their self-respect and so becomes more inclined to coerce them at another place later. Aside from the moral corruption of the public official, the corruption works on the public at large. Most of the popular support for parentalist coercions lies in the notion that *those other people* need to be protected from themselves. By supporting parentalist prohibitions, we develop a habit of demeaning our fellow citizens. Thus some might say that David Kessler and his supporters suffer from an addiction, that Kessler's moral corruption issues from his "coercion dependency."

Liberty and dignity complement one another. Their mutual dependence helps to explain why the price of liberty is vigilance. Encroach on liberty this morning and you cause an erosion of dignity this afternoon, which itself will generate a new encroachment on liberty tomorrow, and so on. If we neglect this multiplier effect, we are apt to underestimate the hazards of coercion.

The Interdependence of Dignity and Individual Responsibility

During the Los Angeles riots, trucker Reginald Denny was dragged from the cab of his truck and beaten. As he lay prone on the street, Damien Williams bounded forward and hurled a rock at his head. The video tape showed that the large rock was thrown with such force that it bounced off Denny's skull. At Williams's trial, the jury acquitted him of attempted murder because "he was caught up in mob violence." Williams's stay in prison may last no longer than four years. Those convicted of murder nowadays stay in prison, on average, for five-and-a-half years.

The jury might rationalize its decision: How can we punish Dr. Jekyll for the deeds of Mr. Hyde? We are loath to see the actions of a Damien Williams as part of an integrated moral force, to hold accountable all his impulses, including the Dr. Jekylls, for the action of a Mr. Hyde. Williams is like a child, and just as we don't accord full liberty to children, we don't put children in prison. After all, Los Angeles was suddenly transformed, the riot a whole new experience. How is one to know how to control himself in astoundingly new situations? Like a child gleefully dropping stones from a balcony, Williams was overcome by the thrill and the turmoil. Heavy punishment would be unfair.

The discounting of dignity now pervades the criminal justice system. Lawyers invoke all manner of syndromes, disorders, and mental illnesses to argue that the defendant is not fully human, that an alien force seized his person, making the human being a mere host. California has no Department of Punishment, but a Department of *Corrections.* The offender is not treated as an integrated moral force that has desecrated the civil order; he is an incompetent, defective, self-contradictory moral force that needs *correcting.* He is not fully human and therefore should not be held fully to account. Indeed, the less dignity the citizens actually have, the more plausible this view becomes.

It seems sometimes we wish to deny all human conflict and

instead pretend to a sustainable, happy, official cooperation. First we deny inner conflict, regarding troublesome impulses as the result of alien "illnesses" or external circumstances. Then we deny the conflict between the offender and society, abnegating punishment for "caring" and "correction." As Thomas Szasz (1990) says, "We appear unable or [un]willing to accept the reality of human conflict. It is never simply man who offends against his fellow man: someone or something—the Devil, mental illness—intervenes, to obscure, excuse, and explain away man's terrifying inhumanity to man" (239). Do we cast ourselves as "caring" and "correcting" in order to deny the conflict within our own breast? Does it testify to our humanity or our hypocrisy that punishment goes out of fashion?

The diminishment of societal dignity erodes individual responsibility and, in turn, the diminishment of responsibility further erodes dignity—hence, we see another avenue of demeanedization. The authorities tell the criminal: "We are not going to punish you. You are blameless for what happened. You did not have the power to prevent it. It happened *to* you. You are a victim of circumstances." The criminal is invited to play the role of a moral invalid.

Instead, to preserve the criminal's dignity, the authorities would say: "What you have done is intolerable to us. You must be punished. That's who we are, and that's who you are. You might change who you are, but that is your business." Then the criminal might come to terms and search his soul for penance.

Danish writer Henrik Stangerup tells a tale of demeanedization in his novel *The Man Who Wanted to Be Guilty* (1982), set in a dystopian Therapeutic State where "it's always the circumstances that dictate our actions." People there have adequate comfort, ample leisure time, and "insurances from head to toe," but no individual responsibility. When trouble arises, citizens call the Helpers, who correct the situation, sometimes with red and green pills. The character Torben is bored and disgusted with life, especially with "the ease with which everybody surrendered to the system." He and his wife had always considered themselves underground dissidents, resisters who would rear their son to

45

know a different ethic. But their spirits have been weakening, especially hers. One evening the crisis of identity erupts in a bitter dispute between them. He recognizes her resignation and foresees a future of meaningless tedium. He becomes drunk and abusive. She calls for the Helpers. He beats her to death.

The last stitch of self-respect Torben could possibly retain lay in being held guilty of his action. But the Helpers tell him that "punishment and guilt are not concepts we use any more." They will care for his future. In Torben's world, the absence of individual responsibility causes such extreme demeanedization that the only way for the hero to proclaim his dignity is to fight for his own guilt and punishment. That is his last chance to affirm the myth of the captain. The novel is a study of affirming one's dignity even when it requires the complete sacrifice of happiness.

Refusing to punish demeans the innocent as well as the guilty. "Pardoning the bad is injuring the good," says Benjamin Franklin. The good stop feeling pride in their behavior when they see the bad indulged. "Maybe they're not bad after all. But then I am no longer good. So why am I bothering?" Indulgence of criminals sends a message of moral emptiness to one and all: "Be not ashamed or proud, for if the captain exists at all he is inane and absurd. Your moral precepts are *mere* myths."

Indulgence carries the same message when it takes the form of welfare-state benefits. Government dispenses aid in an anonymous and arbitrary manner. The benefactors are taxpayers, *forced* to pay. Without voluntary contribution, there can be no gratitude; without gratitude, no generosity. No reciprocity comes about, just a doling out from above. This kind of relationship signifies moral emptiness: the faceless state provides for you regardless of your behavior; no one will ask whether you deserve your benefits. Thence arises the ethic of entitlement. With respect to education and many health benefits, government programs rest on the presumption that individuals or parents cannot care for their own needs or those of their families.

Before creation of the welfare state in America, when mutual aid was pervasive, one of the chief organs of the mutual-aid movement, *The Fraternal Monitor,* decried the rise of govern-

46

ment welfare programs: "The problem of State pensions strikes at the root of national life and character. It destroys the thought of individual responsibility" (21 January 1908; cited in Beito 1990, 720). Welfare benefits place the recipient in the role of helpless supplicant, and the self-reliant person in the role of sucker. Again, pardoning the bad is injuring the good. In contrast, mutual aid rests on reciprocity and the refined use of superior local information. The member down on his luck receives assistance, knowing that it is temporary and given for specific reasons communally recognized as "hard luck." He is not demeaned. The institution would not render assistance to a member if he were "undeserving" (Beito 1990, 1993).

If welfare-state indulgence demeans recipients, it also springs from a collapse of dignity. As Berlin (1969a) observes, "specific forms of the deterministic hypothesis have played an arresting, if limited, role in altering our views of human responsibility" (73). "Structuralism" has always been a major theme of reformers, from Jacob Riis to the New Deal, the Great Society, and most recently Midnight Basketball (Murray 1984, 24–40). In his 1890 tract for housing reform, *How the Other Half Lives,* Riis described tenement buildings and neighborhoods as though the physical structures themselves made residents miserable. Calling for expanded welfare statism in his 1962 *The Other America,* Michael Harrington blamed poverty on "the system." Welfare statists attribute misfortune to "society," "capitalism," "the economy," "patriarchy," "greed," and so on but rarely to the individual experiencing it. Again, as in the case of David Kessler's attitudes toward smokers, the attribution has some truth and justification. As individuals surrender their dignity, they lose ground as authors of their own existence. How can one argue with individuals who say, "Please help me, my captain has fallen overboard and drowned"? Low societal dignity leads to increases in welfare-state indulgences. In a paper entitled, "Hazardous Welfare-State Dynamics" (1995) the Swedish economist Assar Lindbeck argues that the entitlement ethic expands the dole and the dole enhances the entitlement ethic. Another Swedish economist, Nils Karlson (1993, 180), argues that society has gotten stuck in a suboptimal equilibrium in which the state encumbers and crowds out civil society. The thesis conforms to the view of Gordon Tullock (1995) that the growth of government since the 1930s has been a phenomenon of "Bismarckism," or welfare-statism.

Interdependencies Illustrated

If, on the one hand, liberty and dignity are interdependent and, on the other hand, dignity and responsibility are interdependent, then liberty and responsibility are interdependent *by way of dignity.*

Across the top of figure 3 are the connections between Responsibility and Liberty that involve not morals but the dynamics of political economy discussed briefly at the beginning of this article. Below are the connections that involve moral dynamics, working through Dignity. Diminished Liberty causes diminished Dignity. Diminished Dignity points straight back to further diminished Liberty, and to diminished Responsibility. Diminished Responsibility works its effects in similar fashion.

If we were to posit a sudden exogenous shock to Responsibility, the result would be substantial first-round blows to Liberty and Dignity, and then secondary or multiplier effects bouncing through the system. We can illustrate the point with another figure.

Of the connections shown in figure 3, consider only those that point in a clockwise direction: Liberty is a function of Responsibility, which is a function of Dignity, which is a function of Liberty.

Now consider the model shown in figure 4. On the morning of Day 1, Liberty checks the magnitude of Responsibility, and that evening adjusts itself to that magnitude according to the wiggly positively sloped line in the northeast quadrant of the figure. On the morning of Day 2, Dignity checks the magnitude of Liberty, and that evening adjusts itself to that magnitude according to the positively sloped line in the northwest quadrant. This adjusted level of Dignity is reflected from axis to axis in the southwest quadrant; that quadrant is merely a mirror. On the morning of Day 3, Responsibility checks the magnitude of

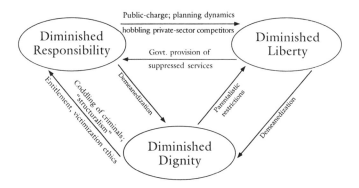

Figure 3. Interdependencies between
Liberty, Dignity, and Responsibility

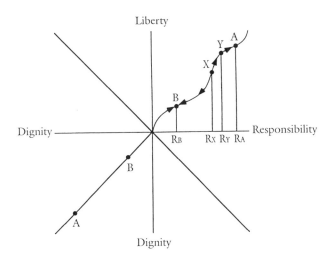

Figure 4. Dynamics of Liberty, Dignity, and Responsibility

49

Dignity, and that evening adjusts itself to that magnitude according to the positively sloped line in the southeast quadrant. Now we've gone full circle, and Liberty is ready again to adjust to Responsibility.

At point A the system is in stable equilibrium. If we pass through the system beginning from point R_A on the Responsibility axis, we keep coming back to point A. Now suppose that somehow an exogenous event causes Responsibility to drop from R_A to R_Y. Liberty and Dignity would drop as well, but as the system cycled, eventually it would return to point A. (The exogenous shock is assumed, implausibly, to last only one period.) It is possible that wounds will heal.

But wounds can also fester and become gangrenous. Suppose that an exogenous event, say the provision of universal governmental Social Security pensions, were to shift Responsibility from R_A to R_X. In this case, as we work through the system we do not move back to A but rather sink further and further until finally we settle at point B. The initial blow to Responsibility amounts to the distance between R_X and R_A, the secondary or multiplier effects to the distance between R_B and R_X. We have stumbled onto the slippery slope, and ultimately are stuck in a system with low Responsibility, low Liberty, and low Dignity.

The formulations of dynamics shown here concord with concerns expressed by Hayek:

> [T]he most important change which extensive government control produces is a psychological change, an alteration in the character of the people. This is necessarily a slow affair, a process which extends not over a few years but perhaps over one or two generations. The important point is that the political ideals of a people and its attitude toward authority are as much the effect as the cause of the political institutions under which it lives. This means, among other things, that even a strong tradition of political liberty is no safeguard if the danger is precisely that new institutions and policies will grad-

ually undermine and destroy that spirit. (Hayek, 1955
Foreword to reissue of 1944, xi–xii)

What Has America Become?

Alexis de Tocqueville perceptively described the American
character (outside the slave states) in the 1830s. His description
probably continued to fit pretty well right up to the twentieth
century. Much that he described Americans might well be glad
to have shed: the naïveté, the insensibility to art and refinement,
the repression of sensual and aesthetic delights, the fervent reli-
giosity, the sanctimony, the bounderism, the oppressive con-
formism. But what of the goodwill, the hope, the self-reliance,
the pride in oneself? Only by straining can we see in Americans
today the following characteristics de Tocqueville ([1835/1840]
1945) saw in the 1830s:

> [A]s soon as the young American approaches manhood,
> the ties of filial obedience are relaxed day by day; master
> of his thoughts, he is soon master of his conduct. . . .
> [T]he son looks forward to the exact period at which he
> will be his own master, and he enters upon his freedom
> without precipitation and without effort, as a possession
> which is his own and which no one seeks to wrest from
> him. . . . In America there is, strictly speaking, no adoles-
> cence: at the close of boyhood the man appears and
> begins to trace out his own path. (2:202–3)

> Long before an American girl arrives at the marriage-
> able age, her emancipation from maternal control
> begins; she has scarcely ceased to be a child when she
> already thinks for herself, speaks with freedom, and acts
> on her own impulse. . . .[T]he vices and dangers of soci-
> ety are early revealed to her; as she sees them clearly, she
> views them without illusion and braves them without
> fear, for she is full of reliance on her own strength, and

her confidence seems to be shared by all around her. . . . Instead, then, of inculcating mistrust of herself, they constantly seek to enhance her confidence in her own strength and character. (2:209–10)

In the United States, as soon as a man has acquired some education and pecuniary resources, either he endeavors to get rich by commerce or industry, or he buys land in the uncleared country and turns pioneer. All that he asks of the state is not to be disturbed in his toil and to be secure in his earnings. (2:263)

When a private individual meditates an undertaking, however directly connected it may be with the welfare of society, he never thinks of soliciting the cooperation of the government; but he publishes his plan, offers to execute it, courts the assistance of other individuals, and struggles manfully against all obstacles. (1:98)

When an American asks for the cooperation of his fellow citizens, it is seldom refused; and I have often seen it afforded spontaneously, and with great goodwill. (2:185)

[I]n no country does crime more rarely elude punishment. The reason is that everyone conceives himself to be interested in furnishing evidence of the crime and in seizing the delinquent. (1:99)

In the United States professions are more or less laborious, more or less profitable; but they are never either high or low: every honest calling is honorable. (2:162)

In the United States hardly anybody talks of the beauty of virtue, but they maintain that virtue is useful and prove it every day. (2:129)

Tocqueville saw a people with self-reliance and self-respect. One of the significant themes of his work is that these traits flowed from the fact that American government at the time was small, decentralized, and permitted much freedom (see esp. vol. 1, chap. 5; vol. 2, book 2, chaps. 4–10). Tocqueville said, "Americans believe their freedom to be the best instrument and surest safeguard of their welfare" (vol. 2, 151).

Do Americans today retain these character traits? The Mexican American writer Richard Rodriguez (1994) remarks on the American spirit: "The notion of self-reliance. The notion of re-creation. More and more I'm sensing that that kind of optimism belongs now to immigrants in this country—certainly to the Mexicans that I meet—and less and less so to the native-born" (36).

All the talk about the breakdown of character in America indicates more than a passing media fad. The entitlement ethic, victimhood, privileges for minorities (who by one calculation constitute 374 percent of the population),[4] the assault on merit, the stigmatization of stigmatization, the proliferation of psychological "disorders," the medicalization of behavior (Szasz 1963; Peele 1989), the abandonment of guilt and punishment, the deterioration of personal responsibility—all seem to be real, and well along in their institutional entrenchment.

A study of the evolution of character in America would be an enormous, wide-ranging undertaking; the changes during just the last few generations have been stupendous. Nonetheless, sweeping aside so many stupendous things in order to air a hypothesis, I submit that the growth of government—a government that increasingly treats citizens as children—has played an important role, even a leading role, in the decline of character. Figure 5 shows federal government expenditures as a percentage of gross national product from 1850 to 1990 (with the war fiscal years 1918–19 and 1940–45 omitted). From the 5 percent range

---

4. The calculation is by Aaron Wildavsky, cited in Sykes (1992, 13).

in 1930, it has climbed steadily (excluding the war years) to reach consistently more than 20 percent in recent years. Adding state and local government outlays would bring the total to about 35 percent. This trend mirrors a massive decline in individual responsibility. At the same time, the decline of liberty has been severe and extensive.

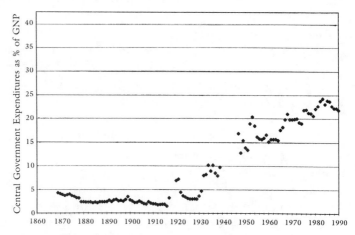

Figure 5. Government Burgeons Beginning in the 1930s

If we are to tell stories that begin with important historical moments, looking to changes in government policy is more plausible than looking to spontaneous changes in moral character. A significant change in government policy might be devised hastily and driven through to political approval; Robert Higgs (1987) has described how this process often accompanies a national crisis. Moral character is obstinate and resilient, but make no mistake: Over time moral character will be altered.

American politics gradually embraced statism, most notably in the 1930s, and major moral decline occurred with a lag. William Julius Wilson (1987, 3) and other scholars have described how, through the 1950s, even in ghetto neighborhoods, common decency, personal responsibility, and public safety remained the norm. Only slowly did erosions of dignity take place, eventually feeding back into indulgence and coercion. Despite short-term fluctuations, it seems safe to say that liberty, dignity, and responsibility have been on a significant slide since the early 1930s and that the problem has become increasingly virulent since the 1960s.

Our problems of declining character have relatively little to do with sexual permissiveness, homosexuality, secularism, paganism, drug use, rock music, rap music, MTV, television violence, Howard Stern, or Hollywood. It is demeanedization of individuals, witnessed and experienced and perpetrated in actual human relations, and legitimized and even celebrated and glorified by officialdom, that really debases and destroys moral character, and that is what the government does on a vast scale with its programs of indulgence and coercion. Moral character is suffocated by the Nanny State, which tells us constantly not to believe in ourselves for we are, and will forever remain, children. Such a fate is exactly what Tocqueville's final chapters warn us against.

A Word to Fellow Travelers

Liberty and individual responsibility are made of the same moral cloth. Both preserve and affirm the dignity of the individual, the myth of self-determination and self-possession, of an integrative self. By corollary, a kinship links coercion, demeanedization, and indulgence. The claim by Hayek that opened this essay—that responsibility and liberty go together historically—can be defended by appeal to the moral dimension of the people. If the argument has merit, it might give pause to those who tend to favor one but not the other. The social democrat should fear for personal freedom when supporting programs of indulgence, and the tory-conservative for responsibility when supporting programs of proscription.

A Reasoned Vigilance for a Worthy Myth

In *The Devil's Dictionary*, Ambrose Bierce defined *liberty* as "one of Imagination's most precious possessions." Even when we try to make her tangible by dressing her with property, consent, and contract, she remains elusive, ambiguous, half in the shadows. Responsibility is more ritual—"*mere* myth!"—and dignity most vaporous of all—"captain of one's soul? Ha!"

The myth speaks for the complexities we cannot explain. The libertarian American founders, such as Thomas Paine and Thomas Jefferson, knew that this triad—liberty, dignity, and responsibility—deserved an eternal vigilance because they knew that each had virtues not easily reduced to cogent argument. When subtle secondary effects abound, effects we sense but do not comprehend in detail, we fail to render their import in words. We manage only judgment, declaration, and action. Sometimes the action is a declaration of our resolve, put in terms of morality, or myths.

The myth of responsibility, for example, holds that the wrongdoer could have refrained from the wrong and hence is "at fault," "to blame," or "guilty." That is the necessary myth that serves clumsily in place of the subtler reasoning that eludes us on the spot or fails to persuade the jury. A student of the deeper reasons for maintaining a system of individual responsibility, such as Hayek (1960), knows better: "We assign responsibility to a man, not in order to say that as he was he might have acted differently, but in order to make him different. . . . In this sense the assigning of responsibility does not involve the assertion of fact. It is rather of the nature of a convention intended to make people observe certain rules" (75).

Myths may help because individuals must be made "to submit to conventions . . . whose justification in the particular instance may not be recognizable" (Hayek 1948, 22). To sustain the convention, to prevent massive free riding by short-term, often compassionate impulses, it must be infused with moral import, mythologized as in: "Men are endowed by their Creator with certain unalienable Rights . . . among these are Life, Liberty, and the pursuit of Happiness." In this connection, Adam Smith wrote:

And thus religion, even in its rudest form, gave a sanction to the rules of morality, long before the age of artificial reasoning and philosophy. That the terrors of religion should thus enforce the natural sense of duty, was of too much importance to the happiness of mankind, for nature to leave it dependent upon the slowness and uncertainty of philosophical researches. (Smith [1790] 1976, 164)

He who scorns a myth merely because it is a myth misses the point, and betrays a poor understanding of his own moral being.

References

Beito, David T. 1990. "Mutual Aid for Social Welfare: The Case of American Fraternal Societies." *Critical Review* 4 (Fall): 709–36.

———. 1993. "Mutual Aid, State Welfare, and Organized Charity: Fraternal Societies and the 'Deserving' and 'Undeserving' Poor, 1900–1930." *Journal of Policy History* 5:419–34.

Berlin, Isaiah. 1969a. "Historical Inevitability." In *Four Essays on Liberty.* New York: Oxford University Press.

———. 1969b. "Two Concepts of Liberty." In *Four Essays on Liberty.* New York: Oxford University Press.

Emerson, Ralph Waldo. 1951. "Self-Reliance." *Essays.* New York: Harper & Row.

Gravett, John. 1993. "Life-Long Smokers Should Welcome Hillary's 'Nico-Tax'." *Excursions,* May 1954.

Hayek, Friedrich A. 1944. *The Road to Serfdom.* Chicago: University of Chicago Press.

———. 1948. "Individualism: True and False." In *Individualism and Economic Order.* Chicago: University of Chicago Press.

———. 1960. *The Constitution of Liberty.* Chicago: University of Chicago Press.

———. 1967. "The Moral Element in Free Enterprise." In *Studies in Philosophy, Politics and Economics.* Chicago: University of Chicago Press.

Higgs, Robert. 1987. *Crisis and Leviathan: Critical Episodes in the Growth of American Government.* New York: Oxford University Press.

Ikeda, Sanford. 1997. *Dynamics of the Mixed Economy: Toward a Theory of Interventionism.* London: Routledge.

Karlson, Nils. 1993. *The State of State: An Inquiry Concerning the Role of Invisible Hands in Politics and Civil Society.* Stockholm: Acta Universitatis Upsaliensis Almquist: Wiksell International.

Kirzner, Israel M. 1985. *Discovery and the Capitalist Process.* Chicago: University of Chicago Press.

Lindbeck, Assar. 1995. "Hazardous Welfare-State Dynamics." *American Economic Review,* Papers and Proceedings, 85 (May): 9–15.

Merton, Robert K. 1957. *Social Theory and Social Structure.* Rev. and enl. Glencoe, Ill.: Free Press.

Mises, Ludwig von. 1978. *Liberalism: A Socio-Economic Exposition.* Kansas City, Mo.: Sheed Andrews and McMeel.

Murray, Charles. 1984. *Losing Ground: American Social Policy, 1950–1980.* New York: Basic Books.

———. 1988. *In Pursuit: Of Happiness and Good Government.* New York: Simon and Schuster.

Peele, Stanton. 1989. *Diseasing of America: Addiction Treatment out of Control.* Boston: Houghton-Mifflin.

Polanyi, Michael. 1958. *Personal Knowledge: Towards a Post-critical Philosophy.* Chicago: University of Chicago Press.

Rawls, John. 1971. *A Theory of Justice.* Cambridge: Harvard University Press.

Riis, Jacob A. 1890. *How the Other Half Lives: Studies Among the Tenements of New York.* New York: C. Scribner's Sons.

Rodriguez, Richard. 1994. "The New, New World: Richard Rodriguez on Culture and Assimilation" (interview). *Reason* 26 (August/September): 35–41.

Rosenthal, Robert, and Lenore Jacobson. 1968. *Pygmalion in the Classroom: Teacher Expectation and Pupils' Intellectual Development.* New York: Holt, Rinehart & Winston.

Schelling, Thomas C. 1984. *Choice and Consequence: Perspectives of an Errant Economist.* Cambridge, Mass.: Harvard University Press.

Smith, Adam. [1790] 1976. *The Theory of Moral Sentiments.* 6th ed. Edited by D. D. Raphael and A. L. Macfie. New York: Oxford University Press.

Stangerup, Henrik. 1982. *The Man Who Wanted to Be Guilty.* Translated by D. Gress-Wright. Salem, N. H.: Marion Boyars, Inc.

Sykes, Charles J. 1992. *A Nation of Victims: The Decay of the American Character.* New York: St. Martin's Press.

Szasz, Thomas. 1963. *Law, Liberty, and Psychiatry.* New York: Macmillan.

———. 1990. *The Untamed Tongue: A Dissenting Dictionary.* La Salle, Ill.: Open Court.

Tocqueville, Alexis de. [1835/1840] 1945. *Democracy in America.* 2 vols. Translated by H. Reeve, F. Bowen, and P. Bradley. New York: Knopf.

Tullock, Gordon. 1995. "Government Growth." *Taiwan Journal of Political Economy* 1:21–36.

Weaver, Carolyn. 1996. "Birth of an Entitlement: Learning from the Origins of Social Security." *Reason* 28 (May): 45–48.

Wildavsky, Aaron. 1988. *Searching for Safety.* New Brunswick, N.J.: Transaction Books.

Wilson, William Julius. 1987. *The Truly Disadvantaged: The Inner City, the Underclass, and Public Policy.* Chicago: University of Chicago Press.

Wooldridge, Adrian. 1997. "Eugenics: The Secret Lurking in Many Nations' Past." *Los Angeles Times* (September 7): pp. M1, M6.

If Government Is So Villainous, How Come Government Officials Don't Seem Like Villains?

The general uncertainty about the prospects of medical treatment is socially handled by rigid entry requirements. These are designed to reduce the uncertainty in the mind of the consumer as to the quality insofar as this is possible. I think this explanation, which is perhaps the naive one, is much more tenable than any idea of a monopoly seeking to increase incomes.

—KENNETH ARROW (1963, 966)

At lunch one day a colleague and I had a friendly argument over occupational licensing. I attacked it for being anticompetitive, arguing that licensing boards raise occupational incomes by restricting entry, advertising, and commercialization. My colleague, while acknowledging anticompetitive aspects, affirmed the need for licensing on the grounds of protecting the consumer from frauds and quacks. In many areas of infrequent and specialized dealing, consumers are not able, *ex ante* or even *ex post,* to evaluate competence. I countered by suggesting voluntary means by which reputational problems might be handled, and by returning to the offensive. I said that in fact the impetus for licensing usually comes from the practitioners, not their customers, and that licensing boards seldom devote their time to ferreting out incompetence but rather simply to prosecuting

Reprinted with changes from *Economics and Philosophy,* 10 (1994), pp. 91–106, by permission of Cambridge University Press 0266–2671/94.

unlicensed practitioners. I mentioned cross-sectional findings, such as those on state licensure, prices, and occupational in-comes. Over-all, I characterized the professional establishment as a group of villains, who set the standards, write the codes, and enforce behavior to enhance their own material well-being. The term economists often use for political operators who seek government-granted resources or privileges is "rent-seekers." The term is advanced especially by Public Choice economists and connotes villainy.

Here, my colleague posed a question that I found very disarming: "Don't you think that the average doctor is honest?" "Don't you think," he said, "that we might get honest doctors on the state licensing board?"

The question disarms one in a great many areas of policy discourse. Anyone who believes that a status quo policy is grossly inefficient, unjust, and inequitable has to come to terms with it. Many feel that gross inefficiency, injustice, and inequity mark the status quo in numerous areas. Are the defenders of the status quo to be set down as liars? Are they all cynics, soullessly clutching their parasitic rents?

Another possibility is to say that our intellectual opponents are misinformed. They believe that what they want is good and what they say is true. But if so, why are they misinformed? Others stand ready to enlighten them, to show them that two plus two is not five. Why aren't they easily straightened out? If it is *we* who are misinformed, why aren't we straightened out? And if both we and they are misinformed, why can't we all at least believe the same error?

Self-Sorting and Screening

Individuals tend to seek out communities and organizations that appeal to their beliefs and values. They gravitate to positions and responsibilities that suit their personal aspirations and ambitions, and in such pursuits they succeed best. In *The United States of Ambition: Politicians, Power, and the Pursuit of Office* (1992), Alan Ehrenhalt argues that the political process tends to select for those who most believe in it and make a career of it. He suggests that one advantage held by the Democratic party (over the Republican party) is that the Democratic party is more thoroughly a party of active government, so it better attracts "people who think running for office is worth the considerable sacrifice it entails" (p. 224). Not only does the political process tend to attract those who believe in it, it also tends to prosper believers.

Sometimes the community holds a belief system, or culture, that does not dovetail with the individual's prior beliefs, in which case the individual must pursue one of the following courses: (a) depart the community; (b) change the culture of the community to suit his beliefs; (c) play the cynic by getting on in the community and supporting its goals while privately rejecting the culture; (d) remain within the community but openly voice a dissenting view; or (e) embrace the culture of the community.

For the stark case of conflicting and firmly held beliefs course (a)—departing the community—is the most likely. Thus self-sorting is a major component of the formation and persistence of organization culture. Economists like Tiebout (1956) and Buchanan (1965) have offered models in which people self-select into communities by "voting with their feet": people select the community with the local collective services, such as swimming pools and security services, that suit their tastes. In the present case people also self-select into communities—communities with suitable collective beliefs.

Course (b), remaking the culture to suit one's own taste, is uncommon. It may occur in young communities when a strong-minded individual finds a position of leadership. Course (c), playing the cynic, is also uncommon when beliefs are squarely in conflict. If the individual just keeps his mouth tight and his mind skeptical, he may feel compromised and frustrated. To play the cynic one must make his behavior neatly chameleon. Few can.

Course (d), open dissent, is not only trying for the individual, it is unsatisfactory to the community and often leads to sanctions or expulsion. Thomas Szasz explains the phenomenon of screening out heterodoxy in the matter of drug policy:

Why do we now lack a right we possessed in the past? ... Why ... does the federal government control our access to some of mankind's most ancient and medically most valuable agricultural products and the drugs derived from them? These are some of the basic questions not discussed in debates on drugs. Why not? Because admission into the closed circle of officially recognized drug-law experts is contingent on shunning such rude behavior. Instead, the would-be debater of the drug problem is *expected to accept, as a premise,* that it is the duty of the federal government to limit the free trade in drugs. All that can be debated is which drugs should be controlled and how they should be controlled." (Szasz 1992, 96; italics added.)

When beliefs are squarely in conflict, the final course of behavior, adapting one's own beliefs, is again uncommon. If the individual tries to surrender his old beliefs for the culture of the community, he may be surrendering precious parts of his selfhood. His old beliefs are like the deep roots of his behavior and habits of mind, so an effort to conform might uproot his moral and intellectual foundation.

When individual beliefs and values are well established prior to participation, therefore, the forces of self-sorting and screening tend to create organizations made up of people with fitting beliefs and values. And, perforce, expertise. Hayek commented on this tendency:

The organizations we have created in these fields [labor, agriculture, housing, education, etc.] have grown so complex that it takes more or less the whole of a person's time to master them. The institutional expert . . . is [frequently] the only one who understands [the institution's] organization fully and who therefore is indispensable. . . . [A]lmost invariably, this new kind of expert has one distinguishing characteristic: he is unhesitatingly in favor of the institutions on which he is expert. This is so not merely because only one who approves of the aims of the institution will have the interest and the patience to master the details, but even more because such an effort would hardly be worth the while of anybody else: the views of anybody who is not prepared to accept the principles of the existing institutions are not likely to be taken seriously and will carry no weight in the discussions determining current policy. . . . [A]s a result of this development, in more and more fields of policy nearly all the recognized "experts" are, almost by definition, persons who are in favor of the principles underlying the policy. . . . The politician who, in recommending some further development of current policies, claims that "all the experts favor it," is often perfectly honest, because only those who favor the development have become experts in this institutional sense, and the uncommitted economists or lawyers who oppose are not counted as experts. Once the apparatus is established, its future development will be shaped by what those who have chosen to serve it regard as its needs. (Hayek 1960, 291)

Belief Plasticity

Firm prior beliefs give rise to self-sorting and screening. But very often a person comes to an organization without strong opinions on matters relating to the organization's purposes. In this case a common course for belief formation is adaptation to the prevailing culture. The individual's lack of opinion usually reflects his innocence of theory about those matters. In the case of the U.S. Department of Agriculture, the theory is about how the agricultural sector works. In the case of the licensing board, the theory is about how licensing affects the practice of the trade.

An individual uses his belief system as an apparatus to cope with his circumstances. Like the steel producer who chooses his inputs to increase his profits, the individual tends to favor certain ideas and theories that render life more comfortable, more pleasant, and more convenient, given his circumstances. His current hopes, information, opportunities, and constraints affect how readily he will take to various ideas and theories.

By "belief plasticity" I mean that individuals would believe different ideas if they were to pursue different goals or were to be inserted into a different cultural environment. The set of ideas that everyone is willing to admit as "the facts" does not always dictate unequivocally beliefs about how the facts relate to one another. This is especially so for social and political affairs. Belief structures are plastic: They are affected by the heat and pressure of everyday experience. People—all people—have different pressures and different yearnings, and these give rise to different beliefs. Were the pressures and yearnings otherwise, so would be the beliefs.

H. L. Mencken demonstrated a lifelong fascination with belief plasticity as it manifested itself in a wide variety of human affairs. What follows is a sample from his *Minority Report* (1956).

> The influenza epidemic of 1919, though it had an enor-
> mous mortality in the United States and was, in fact, the
> worst epidemic since the Middle Ages, is seldom men-
> tioned, and most Americans have apparently forgotten
> it. This is not surprising. The human mind always tries
> to expunge the intolerable from memory, just as it tries
> to conceal it while current. (Mencken 1956, 169)

> [C]onscription in both cases [World Wars I and II]
> involved the virtual enslavement of multitudes of young
> Americans who objected to it. But having been forced
> to succumb, most of them sought to recover their dig-
> nity by pretending that they succumbed willingly and
> even eagerly. Such is the psychology of the war veteran.
> He goes in under duress, and the harsh usage to which
> he is subjected invades and injures his ego, but once he
> is out he begins to think of himself as a patriot and a
> hero. The veterans of all American wars have resisted
> stoutly any effort to examine realistically either the cir-
> cumstances of their service or the body of idea underly-

ing the cause they were forced to serve. Man always seeks to rationalize his necessities—and, whenever possible, to glorify them. (176)

I was once told by a Catholic bishop that whenever a priest comes to his ordinary with the news that he has begun to develop doubts about this or that point of doctrine, the ordinary always assumes as a matter of fact that a woman is involved. It is almost unheard of, however, for a priest to admit candidly that he is a party to a love affair: he always tries to conceal it by ascribing his deserting to theological reasons. The bishop said that the common method of dealing with such situations is to find out who the lady is, and then transfer the priest to some remote place, well out of her reach. (73)

The really astounding thing about marriage is not that it so often goes to smash, but that it so often endures. All the chances run against it, and yet people manage to survive it, and even to like it. The capacity of the human mind for illusion is one of the causes here. Under duress it can very easily convert black into white. It can even convert children into blessings. (3)

Men always try to make virtues of their weaknesses. Fear of death and fear of life both become piety. (47)

The Network Externalities of Culture

Belief systems exhibit network externalities, which is to say, what is best for an individual to believe depends crucially on what his day-to-day coworkers believe. If the individual works in a Christian Fundamentalist church, he will find it awkward to believe that man has evolved from apes. If he works in the U.S. Department of Agriculture, he will find it awkward to believe in the idea that current agricultural policy is absurdly inefficient, unjust, and inequitable. The individual would be out of sync with the actions, attitudes, and goals of the organization. His coworkers have certain underlying beliefs that form a web, and his opinions would upset that web. Coworkers would expect his head to nod when it would like to shake; when they chuckle, he may be inclined to grimace. Were he to defend his beliefs his coworkers may respond with cold seclusion or hot animosity. The smooth workings of the organization would be upset by the cultural impasse. In fact, sheer novelty in behavior, regardless of its nature, can cause resentment. One can become unpopular simply by doing something other than the expected, regardless of what that something is.

Upon entry into the organization the individual is exposed to certain information, embedded within certain ideas. Hence, there is a strong element of information filtering. But in addition, as the individual comes into contact with these ideas, he faces strong incentives to subscribe to the organization line. As Adam Smith wrote in *The Theory of Moral Sentiments*:

> Nature, when she formed man for society, endowed him with an original desire to please, and an original aversion to offend his brethren. She taught him to feel pleasure in their favourable, and pain in their unfavourable, regard. She rendered their approbation most flattering and most agreeable to him for its own sake; and their disapprobation most mortifying and most offensive. (Smith 1790, 116)

To be an effective coworker, to find goodwill among peers, to fetch promotions, the individual must act in accordance with the practices and expectations of the group, and to so act he must think the ideas of the group, and to so think he must, except in cases of dry cynicism, believe the group's beliefs. And coming to believe the community's ideas will be an uncontested choice if the individual is never exposed to competing theories.

Social psychologist Robert Cialdini (1984) sets out several principles that help explain how people come to hold the beliefs they do. One he calls "social proof" or "Truths Are Us." The idea is that people rely on the example of those around them as a cue for appropriate behavior and proper thinking. He explains why television producers use canned laughter, why bartenders "salt" their tip jars with dollar bills, why church ushers sometimes salt their collection baskets, and why evangelical preachers sometimes seed their audience with enthusiasts. He explains how members of a cult can reinforce each other's beliefs, how a victim can suffer a drawn-out vicious assault with dozens of witnesses, not one calling for help, how newspaper reports of suicide can spawn further suicides, and how hundreds of people can line up in orderly and willful fashion to partake of lethal poison, as they did in Jonestown, Guyana, in 1978. If the example of observance by others can decide and reinforce such dreadful beliefs and practices, certainly "social proof" can do much to reinforce the "normal" beliefs and practices of organizations such as duly created government agencies.

An example is the recruiting of individuals to the Unification Church of the Reverend Sun Myung Moon. Here I crib from a discussion of obedience by George Akerlof (1991), who in turn cribs from social psychologist Marc Galanter (1979, 1989). The recruiting process is made up of four steps. As Akerlof explains, "[p]otential recruits are first contacted individually and invited to come to a 2-day, weekend workshop. These workshops are then followed by a 7-day workshop, a 12-day workshop, and membership" (1991, 10). Each step of the program increases in cultural intensity. The structure works beautifully, in conjunction with the self-sorting process, to keep the potential recruit surrounded by other potential recruits who obey and reinforce the practices. The recruit who enters an advanced step of the program does *not* see the resistance that those who have dropped out *would have shown* to the cultural intensification. Nor does he see the resistance that those who *remained* would have shown had they been told in advance what they were to become. As Akerlof puts it, "[b]ecause those who disagree most exit, the dissent necessary for resistance to escalation of commitment does not develop" (1991, 11).

Related here is another principle of belief formation set out by Cialdini: self-consistency and commitment. Because people fancy themselves wise and consistent beings, once a person has taken steps down a certain path, he is receptive to supplementary information and ideas that support the initial decision, and he tends to turn away from information that discredits it. As Adam Smith said,

> The opinion which we entertain of our own character depends entirely on our judgments concerning our past conduct. It is so disagreeable to think ill of ourselves, that we often purposely turn away our view from those circumstances which might render that judgment unfavourable. (Smith 1790, 158)

Isn't it likely that "Truths Are Us" and self-consistency would be operating in the case of those rising to leadership in an organization? Consider the rise of an individual to the state medical licensing board. Most likely such a person must first be a prominent and not-too-innovative member of the profession—bold innovation is often a sign of irreverence. Then perhaps he would find a position in the professional association. After gaining the confidence of influential people in the establishment, he might finally join the state licensing board. Through the stages the individual would be increasingly enveloped by the inner culture of the profession. With each stage outside viewpoints would be cleaved away. Dissenting pleas from powerless outsiders are politely dismissed and privately derogated. Herbert Simon (1976, xvi) says, a person "does not live for months or years in a particular position in an organization, exposed to some streams of communication, shielded from others, without the most profound effects upon what he knows, believes, attends to, hopes, wishes, emphasizes, fears, and proposes." The incentive to maintain and advance one's prior commitments to the profession would be enhanced; to challenge or innovate would cause disruptions both personally and in the day-to-day workings of the organization. As James Q. Wilson (1989, 110) says, "the perceptions supplied by an organizational culture sometimes can

70

lead an official to behave not as the situation requires but as the culture expects." And only those amenable to the necessary commitments would climb the ladder.

The same argument applies to any organization, whether communal, commercial, nonprofit, or governmental. But the most important application is to government organizations, since they have the most far-reaching and peremptory power. As Hayek (1944, 104) said, "the power which a multiple millionaire, who may be my neighbor and perhaps my employer, has over me is very much less than that which the smallest *fonctionnaire* possesses who wields the coercive power of the state and on whose discretion it depends whether and how I am to be allowed to live or to work." Government officials wield incomparably greater power than do businessmen, and they exercise it with much greater likelihood of calamitous consequence. One need only consider petty officials at the FDA who routinely make decisions that prevent suffering individuals from being helped by new drugs.

The network of beliefs within a community may be related to the idea of "path dependence," or "lock-in," discussed by Paul David (1985; see also the important work of Liebowitz and Margolis, 1990). A path-dependent process is one that reinforces and steers itself once it has begun. Once members of a primitive society begin using copper as a medium of exchange, everyone joins in the use of copper. Once one particular textbook becomes customary for the Introductory Economics sequence, each professor has the incentive to stick with that textbook. Once the copper or textbook gets a foothold, it becomes "locked in"; that is, the arrangement is the reason for its own perpetuation. The moral of the story is that perhaps the original foothold was made in an adventitious or shortsighted way—gold actually would serve better than copper, or some textbook other than the one chosen—but once down the path a reversal is difficult to make. The result may be perpetual suboptimality. Hats off to the French rationalists who forced their countrymen to use the metric system—and chalk one up for *dirigisme*.

David explains that path dependence occurs when three

features are present: technical interrelatedness, economies of scale, and quasi-irreversibility. Although David explores technological systems, the ideas can be applied to belief systems within communities or organizations. The first feature, technical interrelatedness, is the need for compatibility among members of the network. Again, network externalities are clearly exhibited by the belief system of a community. A common apprehension of ends, values, and opportunities is crucial to the efficiency of the community. A mind with the wrong beliefs can disrupt the smooth working of an organization in much the same way that a stretch of railroad track with the wrong gauge can disrupt the smooth passing of a locomotive train.

David's second aspect of path dependence, economies of scale, says that the more that system A is adopted within the community, the easier it will be to bring an additional individual into system A. Learning and using the system gets easier the more the system is used. This principle would seem to apply to belief systems. The more that one's coworkers share a common belief system, the more solidified and imposing that system will be. Beliefs that are very common come to be taken as "common sense." Basic notions become second nature, and, building on basic notions, community practices produce a mortar of supplementary beliefs, procedures, and rituals. Questioning the community's common sense is sure to gain one unpopularity. Often basic cultural premises are so uncontroversial that they go wholly unstated and unchallenged (see Kuran 1995). Truths are us.

When most of the people working in an organization share a belief system, newcomers are quickly socialized and they then help solidify that system. In an organization, then, some system will come to dominate the thinking of the workers, just as in a "Polya urn scheme" some color will come to dominate the balls in the urn.[1] To change the metaphor, those who percolate

---

1. David (1985, 335) explains the Polya urn scheme: "an urn containing balls of various colors is sampled with replacement, and every drawing of a ball of a specified color results in a second ball of the same color being returned to the

through the cultural filter of an organization afterward might *become part of the filter* and enhance its purifying properties.

The third feature of path dependence is quasi-irreversibility of investments, which is to say, the costs of the original capital (whether animal, mineral, or intellectual) are at least partially sunk; switching to a new capital good would entail further investment. The first two features of path-dependent systems may present a sufficiently severe collective action problem to account for the persistence of suboptimal outcomes, but quasi-irreversibility reinforces the difficulty of jumping to a better path once the community has started down a suboptimal one. In the case of belief systems, Cialdini and Adam Smith have told us that individuals become attached to their beliefs. New experiences that compel one to change his mind can be both depressing, since his old intellectual investments will no longer serve him, and heartbreaking, since his old investments will have come to hold personal and sentimental value. Such new experiences can be tragic, much the way a conflagration can be. Hence the saying, "Ignorance is bliss." Like installing a smoke detector, sometimes we program ourselves to detect and avert new experiences and new arguments because they would jeopardize the peace of mind that our current beliefs afford us. And sometimes we refrain from challenging the beliefs of another, not out of fear of jeopardizing our own peace of mind, but out of a compassionate impulse to safeguard his.[2]

In an important work, Timur Kuran has modeled public

---

urn: the probabilities that balls of specified colors will be added are therefore increasing (linear) functions of the proportions in which the respective colors are represented within the urn." It has been shown that "the proportional share of one of the colors will, with probability one, converge to unity."

2. "The loss of faith, to many minds, involves a stupendous upset—indeed, that upset goes so far in some cases that it results in something hard to distinguish from temporary insanity. It takes a long while for a naturally trustful person to reconcile himself to the idea that after all God will not help him. He feels like a child thrown among wolves. For this reason I have always been chary about attempting to shake religious faith. It seems to me that the gain to truth that it involves is trivial when set beside the damage to the individual" (Mencken 1956, 141).

opinion as a process of path dependence and multiple equilibria. In his main model individuals are endowed with "private preferences" and then choose their "public preferences," or outwardly displayed preferences. Which preference one finds most advantageous to display depends, due to the peer effect and social incentives, on what others are displaying.[3] Thus suboptimality might become locked in, or we might witness sudden revolutionary swings in outward preferences—in the manner of the French, Russian, Iranian, and East European revolutions. Kuran is interested especially in the attitudes of overall society, *where exit is very difficult;* hence his focus on preference *falsification.* I am more interested in beliefs within a subgroup, where exit is easier, and hence my focus on belief adaptation and self-sorting. But it should be noted that Kuran also gives much attention to the possibility of the *private* preferences being dependent on the path, thereby highlighting the idea that all belief formation is a contingent social process.

Much earlier William James wrote of belief systems as a social process and acknowledged the possibility of lock-in. He said:

> Our ancestors may at certain moments have struck into ways of thinking which they might conceivably not have found. But once they did so, and after the fact, the inheritance continues. When you begin a piece of music in a certain key, you must keep the key to the end. You may alter your house *ad libitum,* but the ground-plan of the first architect persists— you can make great changes, but you can not change a Gothic church into a Doric temple. You may rinse and rinse the bottle, but you can't get the taste of the medicine or whiskey that first filled it wholly out. (James 1963 [1907], 75)

---

3. "[A]n individual, when he joins a crowd, whether of life-long Democrats, Methodists or professors, sacrifices his private judgment in order to partake of the power and security that membership gives him" (Mencken 1987 [1921], 154).

74

James goes on to explain that what we call "common sense" is in fact the product of circumstances and, quite possibly, historical accidents. Sometimes we find ourselves in conversations in which our "common sense" and the other guy's "common sense" cannot find much in common.

As for the individual who stumbles into a community and finds herself traveling a path involving elaborate new beliefs, the story is a case of what the pragmatist philosopher Richard Rorty calls "contingency." In *Contingency, Irony, and Solidarity* (1989) Rorty describes the broad terms of social life as set, not only by necessities or human deliberation, but also by blind contingency. Who we are is not essential, but accidental, the result of what family we were born into, what theories we were exposed to, what schools we went to, what jobs we landed, the time and place of our existence. Not only could our physical doings have been otherwise, but the *way we describe* physical doings, including our own, could also have been otherwise. Culture not only generates incentives to believe in certain ideas rather than others, it provides the ideas among which we choose our beliefs. Rorty's view, like James's, is uncompromisingly anti-essentialist—there can be no metacultural description, only cultural ones—and hence he preaches concession to ironism.

There are, then, several distinct principles that help explain uniformity in behavior or belief: self-sorting and screening (noted by Akerlof 1991), network externalities and belief adaptation (noted by Mencken and discussed in the context of technology, not cognition, by David), filtered information (noted by Simon), imitation based on uncertainty (congruent with Cialdini and developed by Bikhchandani et al. 1992), preferences to conform (noted by Cialdini, Adam Smith, and Kuran), and sanctions on deviants (discussed by Kuran and noted by Mencken).

The Genealogy of Organization Culture

If organization culture exhibits lock-in, there remains the question of which path will emerge. Path dependence tells us that the enduring equilibrium may have very adventitious origins, so in that sense there may be no way to generalize about what sort of equilibrium results. But the consideration of origins and of certain incentives that operate irrespective of cultural specifics may permit some generalization.

A relativist tradition beginning perhaps with Protagoras and including such thinkers as Machiavelli, La Rochefoucauld, Vico, Mandeville, Marx, Spencer, Nietzsche, Sumner, Mencken, and Burke maintains that interest drives social mores, and social mores drive morality. Members of a community come to call "good" any behavior that promotes the interests of the community and "bad" any that damages it. By a process of legitimation, interest is transformed into propriety and justice. Thereafter community members obey not only their interest but also their conscience. When a community is isolated the culture governs all and the society is tranquil in its practices. But if the community is embedded within a larger society, the way a government agency is, the cultural development of the agency is constrained by the interests and theories of the larger society. The interests of the society may in fact be bred into the members of the agency, so the agency may faithfully serve the greater good. But there will be some interests particular to the agency and its members.

Everyone wants more comfort and wealth. Almost everyone wants recognition, prestige, eminence, and power. We want a sense of significance, importance, potency. We feel important when we can believe a story in which we get to play the hero. We want to take credit for both the good and the greatness achieved. We want to not hurt colleagues and associates near to us. As Akerlof (1989, 13) says, people "choose beliefs which make them feel good about themselves." Call it the *self-exaltation principle*. It will sometimes conflict with the conscience, but the plasticity of belief will to some extent permit the conscience to accommodate self-exaltation even when onlookers perhaps feel it shouldn't. Government officials, especially high-ranking ones, find comfort and prestige in their position. They will come to find legitimacy as well. They like to see their agency's actions as the cause of achievement, and themselves the cause of the agency's actions. The self-sorting and screening effects tend to prevent someone with strongly contrary views from entering the community; most of the others join the community and embrace the culture, which claims importance and legitimacy. The propensity of self-exaltation is universal enough that we can expect it to be one of the forces shaping cultural development— that means the pursuit of expanded power and a willful reluctance to surrender it.

We might also generalize on the basis of agency founding. We find what may be called the *founding principle*: the founding of the agency gives a cultural foothold to certain theories and goals that will to a great extent determine the belief system into the future. The push for occupational licensing was fueled by doctors seeking, often quite unabashedly, to limit competition, and justified by the theory that society needs protection from quacks. The Department of Agriculture grew out of the theory that farmers were getting a bad shake and the goal became arranging price supports and subsidies. The public school system was rationalized by the need for instruction and the goal of public instruction persists. A mountain of literature has persuaded many people that the public school system is cause for great remorse, but few in the education establishment have been persuaded.[4] As the Viennese social critic Karl Kraus asks, "Who is going to cast out an error to which he has given birth and replace it with an adopted truth?" (1990, 114). Those who favor laissez faire and doubt the efficacy of government are likely to see badness persisting in the cultural systems of government agencies, since those agencies were founded to abridge laissez faire.

The self-exaltation principle gives reason to believe that the culture of government agencies will favor expanded government power, and the founding principle gives another reason to expect the culture to be highly statist. Although outside theories

---

4. Chubb and Moe (1990, 46) say the following of those in the public school establishment: "Although traditionally they have tried to portray themselves as nonpolitical experts pursuing the greater good, they are in fact a powerful constellation of special interests dedicated to hierarchical control and the formalization of education."

seep into the agency through its many holes and cracks, given belief plasticity and the network externalities within the agency, libertarians have reason for saying that government officials and allied parties often pursue bad policies but believe in their goodness. Thomas Jefferson would agree that the irreproachable honesty of the members of the medical licensing board is no evidence of beneficence:

> It would be dangerous delusion were a confidence in the men of our choice to silence our fears for the safety of our rights; that confidence is everywhere the parent of despotism. Free government is founded in jealousy and not in confidence; it is jealousy, and not confidence which prescribes limited constitutions, to bind down those whom we are obliged to trust with power. (Kentucky Resolutions, November 16, 1798)

Example: "The Culture of Spending"

James L. Payne has written a book about Congress that emphasizes belief plasticity and network externalities in cultural systems. He argues that the beliefs of congresspeople "will be affected by the information and opinions they are exposed to day after day." In fact, Congress "is overwhelmed by the advocates of government programs." Payne, who himself spent much time in the bowels of the persuasion process on Capitol Hill while researching his book, provides data showing that in the persuasion process the ratio of pro-spending voices to anti-spending voices is more than 100:1 (1991, 13). Even though one might understand from afar why only pro-spending interests seek the ear of Congress, in the barrage of pro-spending testimony the human mind simply succumbs to the senses and begins to accept what it hears. How unpleasantly and unremittingly jaundiced one must become otherwise! Like the poles that form the cone-shaped frame of a tepee, the lobbyists, agency staffers, media personnel, aides, and congresspeople all reinforce one another's beliefs. The principle of mutual reinforcement is nicely captured by an aphorism of Karl Kraus, who wrote bitterly against the First World War: "How is the world ruled and led to war? Diplomats lie to journalists and believe these lies when they see them in print" (1990 [ca 1918], 81).

The culture of spending on Capitol Hill, explains Payne, revolves around two central premises: (i) "the philanthropic fallacy," or the virtual nonexistence of alternative uses for the citizen's tax dollar, and (ii) the efficacy of government programs. Regarding the "philanthropic fallacy," Payne highlights how the will to self-exalt shapes beliefs:

> Everyone wants to have a high opinion of himself. . . . When the congressman comes to Washington, he is surrounded by beneficiaries and claimants who are pleading for his "help." He is strongly invited to accept the role of philanthropist, strongly encouraged to believe that he has assisted people and left the country better off by funding government programs. . . . This high self-opinion would be directly threatened if the donor of funds [that is, the taxpayers] were brought into the picture. As soon as one recognizes that in order to help some people you have to hurt others, much of the glow goes out of being a congressman. For this reason, congressmen are reluctant to face the opportunity-cost issue. (Payne, 1991, 53)

Regarding the presumption of government efficacy, Payne says, "Congressmen tend to trust that government programs actually accomplish their intended purpose. They suppose that programs to 'help farmers,' or 'help science,' or 'help the poor' actually do what they are intended to do. One has to work long and hard pointing out defects in each scheme to overcome this basic credulity" (Ibid., 163). Payne highlights the Truths-Are-Us nature of these beliefs: "For most congressmen, spending programs are cultural 'givens,' an aspect of their environment that they accept without question"[5] (Ibid., 173). In discussing the source of program evaluation information, Payne remarks on the role of self-sorting and screening: "personnel in government agencies will tend to believe that what their agency does is useful. . . . An official who believed his program was useless or harmful would probably weed himself out of the agency even before the system expelled him" (Ibid., 36).[6]

Payne explains that the congressperson's beliefs are, to a great extent, adopted only once the politician enters the culture of spending:

> When the innocent enters policy realms armed only with the general idea that "spending is bad," he is easily seduced, for this abstract homily is overpowered by visions of starving millions and eroding continents. The situation is not unlike sending a farm boy to town and telling him to "keep out of trouble." Because he is unaware of all the appealing and subtle forms "trouble" can take in specific instances, this general advice is practically worthless. (Payne 1991, 158)

Payne supports his theory with a variety of forms of evidence, to show that congresspersons of both parties become substantially more pro-spending the longer they dwell in "the culture of

---

5. Hayek (1960, 112) makes the following related remark: "For the practical politician concerned with particular issues, these beliefs are indeed unalterable facts to all intents and purposes. It is almost necessary that he be unoriginal, that he fashion his program from opinions held by large numbers of people. The successful politician owes his power to the fact that he moves within the accepted framework of thought, that he thinks and talks conventionally. It would be almost a contradiction in terms for a politician to be a leader in the field of ideas."

6. Although watchdog agencies like the Congressional Budget Office and the General Accounting Office are supposed to challenge the overly convenient beliefs of lawmakers, such agencies in fact are influenced by the lawmakers themselves and are rather ineffective (Payne, 66–70).

spending." (There is an unresolved scholarly debate on this question.[7])

Other theories of congressional spending, such as pork-barrel politics, log-rolling, and vote maximization, give the impression that politicians must be rather venal characters. Payne gives a different impression:

> The high-spending congressman does not feel he is a crook. He does not perceive that he is taking money away from some people to give it to others. He lives in a world of euphemism where the federal government "generates" a "general revenue" that well-intentioned "public servants" can spend to "promote the general welfare." (Payne 1991, 166)

---

7. One type of evidence used by Payne is longitudinal data, tracking over time congresspersons' voting records on spending bills, and he presents evidence of congresspeople becoming, beginning with their second year, increasingly in favor of spending. Aka, Reed, Schansberg, and Zhu (1996) also do a longitudinal study and find that the "culture of spending" results dissolves for a sample size larger than what Payne used. Payne has noted in correspondence, however, that the Aka et al. analysis does not properly control for several features of the problem, including prior government experience by congresspeople (in which they have been immersed in a culture of spending before their freshman term), the "apprentice effect" concerning the common peculiarity of first-year voting patterns, the phenomenon of a congressman like Ted Kennedy maxing out on the spending barometer and therefore not evidencing a tendency to become more in favor of spending over time, and the way national-defensive bills are handled. In private conversation with the author, Eric Schansberg has expressed a recognition of the conceptual validity of these points in relation to his own study, and seems to feel that the question of a correlation is still an open one. It should be noted that the general validity of Payne's culture hypothesis really does not depend on there being a correlation between voting-for-spending and tenure-in-Congress (although such a correlation would be nice evidence for it). If the acculturation occurs prior to arrival in office (for example, in prior government service or during the campaign), the correlation will not be found, but the culture theory might nonetheless help us understand why spending is as popular as it is among congresspeople. I hope researchers try to refine the empirical investigation of the culture hypothesis.

Payne's persuasion hypothesis answers many questions that other theories do not, including the most immediate one of why politicians, even with all their platitudes, seem more-or-less sincere in their efforts.[8]

Conclusion: They Are Honest and Rent-Seeking

> ... and they are not the less quacks when they happen to be quite honest.
>
> Mencken (1919, 80)

> The annual produce of the land and labour of England ... is certainly much greater than it was ... a century ago. ... [Y]et during this period, five years have seldom passed away in which some book or pamphlet has not been published ... pretending to demonstrate that the wealth of the nation was fast declining, that the country was depopulated, agriculture neglected, manufacturers decaying, and trade undone. Nor have these publications been all party pamphlets, the wretched offspring of falsehood and venality. Many of them have been written by very candid and very intelligent people; who wrote nothing but what they believed, and for no other reason but because they believed it.
>
> Smith (1776, 327)

The proximate spark igniting me to write the present paper was my friendly argument over occupational licensing. This paper is an extended response to my colleague's challenge invok-

---

8. One can imagine methods of studying belief effects in organizations. For example, one might learn about self-sorting effects by interviewing those who depart the organization and those who do not, or new arrivals versus veterans. One might learn from studying massive shifts in personnel, or in the creation of new subunits, staffed either by insiders or outsiders, or by a change in where the agency reports its activities.

ing the honesty of the average doctor. I have said that I found his point disarming; also I found it a little naïve. Wouldn't we expect the members of a state licensing board to be exceptional *and sincere* advocates of the cause? Are we surprised to learn that the A.M.A. opposes midwife birthing, the right to die, and the relaxation of prescription requirements on drugs? Are we surprised that the education establishment vociferously opposes school vouchers? Are we surprised that civil engineers champion rail transit projects, that university professors champion the value of higher education, or defense officials, the need for a strong military? Of course not, nor do we seriously doubt their sincerity. Although I firmly believe that occupational licensing serves existing practitioners and disserves the public at large, I do not suspect venality. It does not surprise me that a leading student of the subject reports that, "Despite the many opportunities that exist for bribery and corruption in the granting of licenses and deciding disciplinary cases, the record is amazingly clean."[9] I hope that the present paper lends structure and refinement to the intuitions held in this regard.

Does the culture theory suggested here conflict with theories that portray political actors as cynical egotists? Not necessarily. We just need to make clear that when we offer a description based on assumptions of self-seeking behavior, we present the description as one, simplified description of the matter, and *not* the one that the political participants themselves believe. When Milton Friedman (1953, 19) said we can describe the growth of a plant as behavior aimed at maximizing sunlight exposure subject to constraints, he certainly was not saying that the plant saw it that way. Baldly cynical theories (the Public Choice perspective) can give useful insights into the behavior of real people who are in fact not cynical. Malady does not imply malevolence, just as benefit does not imply benevolence. Some consequences are unintended.

As investigators of government failure, we may toggle

---

9. Shimberg 1982, p. 9. There is much scholarly literature on occupational licensing, almost all of it critical to one degree or another. A good survey is Hogan (1983).

between what Sanford Ikeda distinguishes as the *deception thesis,* which he associates with Public Choice economists, and the *error thesis,* which he associates with Austrian economics. Austrian political economy, says Ikeda, grants if only for the sake of argument, scruple, and public interest on the part of government officials (Ikeda 1997b). The present paper suggests that the two approaches are not necessarily beginning with different assumptions, but rather may be describing the same assumptions in two different ways (cf. Ikeda 1997a, 114, 119, 148, 149, 240). The appropriateness of each description depends in part on one's discourse situation and rhetorical purpose.

Sometimes it is appropriate to incriminate government officials. For the cynical and irresponsible ones, we might deem their behavior reprehensible. It will depend on how we delimit responsible beliefs given the individual's personal constraints. But I suggest that we strain to see how bad conclusions might have been reached by thought processes that were ordinarily honest and good-willed. Libertarians should meet and join institutions of power, they should cooperate and negotiate with those in power. To do that effectively, we must tell ourselves that it is up to the wise to undo the damage done by the merely good.[10]

No matter how disagreeable we may find the culture of another community, there is no profit in addressing its members strictly on our terms. As Payne says, the "congressman will not be persuaded by lobbyists who believe he is a dishonest cad" (166). If the political-intellectual-academic arena is one of cultural struggle, success is not called triumph or victory, but persuasion.

---

10. I find this saying in the good and wise book by Wildavsky (1988, 91).

References

Aka, Arsene, Robert Reed, Eric Schansberg, and Zhen Zhu. 1996. "Is There a 'Culture of Spending' in Congress?" *Economics and Politics* 8:191–211.

Akerlof, George A. 1989. "The Economics of Illusion." *Economics and Politics* 1:1–15.

———. 1991. "Procrastination and Obedience." *American Economic Review* 81:1–19.

——— and William T. Dickens. 1982. "The Economic Consequences of Cognitive Dissonance." *American Economic Review* 72:307–19.

Arrow, Kenneth. 1963. "Uncertainty and the Economics of Medical Care." *American Economic Review* 53:941–67.

Bikhchandani, Sushil, David Hirshleifer, and Ivo Welch. 1992. "A Theory of Fads, Fashion, Custom, and Cultural Change as Informational Cascades." *Journal of Political Economy* 100:992–1027.

Buchanan, James M. 1965. "An Economic Theory of Clubs." *Economica* (February): 1–14.

Cialdini, Robert B. 1984. *Influence: How and Why People Agree to Things.* New York: William Morrow and Co.

Chubb, John E. and Terry M. Moe. 1990. *Politics, Markets & America's Schools.* Washington, D.C.: The Brookings Institution.

David, Paul A. 1985. "Clio and the Economics of QWERTY." *American Economic Review* 75:332–37.

Ehrenhalt, Alan. 1992. *The United States of Ambition: Politicians, Power, and the Pursuit of Office.* New York: Times Books.

Friedman, Milton. 1953. "The Methodology of Positive Economics." In *Essays in Positive Economics.* Chicago: University of Chicago Press.

Galanter, Marc. 1989. *Cults: Faith, Healing, and Coercion.* New York: Oxford University Press.

——— et al. 1979. "The 'Moonies': A Psychological Study of Conversion and Membership in a Contemporary Religious Sect." *American Journal of Psychiatry* 136:165–70.

Hayek, Friedrich A. 1944. *The Road to Serfdom.* Chicago: University of Chicago Press.

———. 1960. *The Constitution of Liberty.* Chicago: University of Chicago Press.

Ikeda, Sanford. 1997a. *Dynamics of the Mixed Economy: Toward a Theory of Interventionism.* London: Routledge.

———. 1997b. "How Compatible Are Public Choice and Austrian Political Economy? Tales of Deception and Error." Mss. Presented at the 1997 meetings of the Southern Economic Association.

Hogan, Daniel B. 1983. "The Effectiveness of Licensing: History, Evidence, and Recommendations," *Law and Human Behavior* 7:117–38.

James, William. 1963. *Pragmatism and Other Essays.* New York: Washington Square Press.

Kraus, Karl. 1990. *Half-Truths and One-and-a-Half Truths,* trans. and ed. by Harry Zohn. Chicago: University of Chicago Press.

Kuran, Timur. 1995. *Private Truths, Public Lies: The Social Consequences of Preference Falsification.* Cambridge, Mass.: Harvard University Press.

Liebowitz, S. J., and Stephen E. Margolis. 1990. "The Fable of the Keys." *Journal of Law and Economics* 33:1–25.

Mencken, H. L. 1919. *Prejudices: First Series.* New York: Alfred A. Knopf.

———. 1956. *Minority Report: H. L. Mencken's Notebooks.* New York: Alfred A. Knopf.

———. 1987. *H. L. Mencken's Smart Set Criticism,* ed. William H. Nolte. Washington, D.C.: Gateway Editions.

Payne, James L. 1991. *The Culture of Spending: Why Congress Lives Beyond Our Means.* San Francisco: ICS Press.

Rorty, Richard. 1989. *Contingency, Irony, and Solidarity.* New York: Cambridge University Press.

Shimberg, Benjamin. 1982. *Occupational Licensing: A Public Perspective.* Princeton, N.J.: Educational Testing Service.

Simon, Herbert. 1976. *Administrative Behavior,* 3rd ed. New York: Free Press.

Smith, Adam. 1776. *The Wealth of Nations.* New York: Modern Library, 1937.

Szasz, Thomas. 1992. *Our Right to Drugs: The Case for a Free Market.* New York: Praeger.

Tiebout, Charles M. 1956. "A Pure Theory of Local Expenditures," *Journal of Political Economy* 84 (February): 416–24.

Wildavsky, Aaron. 1988. *Searching for Safety.* New York: Transaction Books.

Wilson, James Q. 1989. *Bureaucracy: What Government Agencies Do and Why They Do It.* New York: Basic Books.

Index

The Foundation for Economic Education

COUNCIL OF SCHOLARS

$8.50 U.S.

The Foundation for Economic Education, Inc.
30 South Broadway
Irvington-o...   ...33
(914) 591-...   ...10

All About Drums

Greg Roza

Rosen Classroom Books & Materials
New York

Published in 2003 by The Rosen Publishing Group, Inc.
29 East 21st Street, New York, NY 10010

Copyright © 2003 by The Rosen Publishing Group, Inc.

Book Design: Haley Wilson

Photo Credits: Cover (background), p. 1(background) © Bob Winsett/Corbis; cover (drums), pp. 1 (drums), 3, 5, 8, 9, 11, 12, 12–13, 14 © Eyewire; pp. 4 (top, bottom), 7 © SuperStock; p. 10 (background) © J. Contreras Chacel/International Stock; p. 10 (top) © Scott Barrow/International Stock; p. 10 (bottom) © Phylis Picardi/International Stock.

ISBN: 0-8239-6381-0
6-pack ISBN: 0-8239-9563-1

Manufactured in the United States of America

Contents

4

Drums and Drumming

Have you ever played a drum? Drums are the oldest **instruments** (IN-struh-ments). Most music groups have someone who plays the drums. Drummers help keep an even beat for other musicians to follow.

Drums come in many sizes and shapes. Just about every country in the world has its own kind of drum.

Drums of the Past

People began making and using drums thousands of years ago. The oldest drum we know of was made about 8,000 years ago! We think the first drums were parts of **hollow** trees covered with animal skin that was pulled tight. People made sound with these drums by hitting the skin with their hands.

Today, drums are often made with wood and animal skins, just as they were thousands of years ago.

The Parts of Drums

All drums have at least two parts, the shell and the head. The shell is shaped like a bowl or **tube** and is commonly made of wood or **metal**. The head is made of a very thin piece of **plastic** or animal skin pulled tightly over one end of the shell.

The head can be held
on the shell with nails, glue,
or string. Some drums have
heads over both ends of
the shell.

head

shell

pedal

Some drums have a pedal that tightens and
loosens the head. This pedal changes the
sound the drum makes.

9

Drums make sound when we hit them. Instruments that make sound when they are hit are called **percussion** (per-KUH-shuhn) instruments. Most drums are played by hitting the drum's head with a stick or **mallet**. Some drums, like **bongos**, are played by hitting the drum's head with your hands.

Drummers use their hands or different kinds of sticks to make different sounds with their drums.

11

bass drum

tambourine

How Drums Make Sound

When you hit the head of a drum, the head shakes very quickly and makes the sound you hear. The shell of the drum keeps the head tight. The tighter the head, the higher the sound of the drum.

The shell can also make the drum's sound louder and longer. The bigger the shell, the deeper the sound of the drum.

A bass drum is a big drum with a low sound. A tambourine is a small drum with a high sound.

Other Uses for Drums

Some people use drums during **religious** services. Drums have also been used to send messages to people who are far away and to give orders to **soldiers** during battles.

Today, drums are still used by many people all over the world—for work and for fun!

Glossary

bongo   A small drum that is usually held between the knees of a seated drummer and played with the hands. Bongos come in pairs.

hollow   With nothing on the inside.

instrument   Something used to make music.

mallet   A stick with a thick, padded end used to play a drum.

metal   A hard substance such as iron, gold, or silver.

percussion   A kind of instrument that makes sound when it is hit.

plastic   Something man-made that can be shaped into many different things, like bottles, toys, and computers.

religious   Honoring a god or gods.

soldier   Someone who is in an army.

tube   A long, round, hollow shape.

Index